CS-4   GENERAL APTITUDE AND ABILITIES SERIES

This is your
PASSBOOK for...

Civil Service Secretary

Test Preparation Study Guide
Questions & Answers

COPYRIGHT NOTICE

This book is SOLELY intended for, is sold ONLY to, and its use is RESTRICTED to individual, bona fide applicants or candidates who qualify by virtue of having seriously filed applications for appropriate license, certificate, professional and/or promotional advancement, higher school matriculation, scholarship, or other legitimate requirements of education and/or governmental authorities.

This book is NOT intended for use, class instruction, tutoring, training, duplication, copying, reprinting, excerption, or adaptation, etc., by:

1) Other publishers
2) Proprietors and/or Instructors of "Coaching" and/or Preparatory Courses
3) Personnel and/or Training Divisions of commercial, industrial, and governmental organizations
4) Schools, colleges, or universities and/or their departments and staffs, including teachers and other personnel
5) Testing Agencies or Bureaus
6) Study groups which seek by the purchase of a single volume to copy and/or duplicate and/or adapt this material for use by the group as a whole without having purchased individual volumes for each of the members of the group
7) Et al.

Such persons would be in violation of appropriate Federal and State statutes.

PROVISION OF LICENSING AGREEMENTS – Recognized educational, commercial, industrial, and governmental institutions and organizations, and others legitimately engaged in educational pursuits, including training, testing, and measurement activities, may address request for a licensing agreement to the copyright owners, who will determine whether, and under what conditions, including fees and charges, the materials in this book may be used them. In other words, a licensing facility exists for the legitimate use of the material in this book on other than an individual basis. However, it is asseverated and affirmed here that the material in this book CANNOT be used without the receipt of the express permission of such a licensing agreement from the Publishers. Inquiries re licensing should be addressed to the company, attention rights and permissions department.

All rights reserved, including the right of reproduction in whole or in part, in any form or by any means, electronic or mechanical, including photocopying, recording, or by any information storage and retrieval system, without permission in writing from the Publisher.

Copyright © 2024 by
National Learning Corporation

212 Michael Drive, Syosset, NY 11791
(516) 921-8888 • www.passbooks.com
E-mail: info@passbooks.com

PUBLISHED IN THE UNITED STATES OF AMERICA

PASSBOOK® SERIES

THE *PASSBOOK® SERIES* has been created to prepare applicants and candidates for the ultimate academic battlefield – the examination room.

At some time in our lives, each and every one of us may be required to take an examination – for validation, matriculation, admission, qualification, registration, certification, or licensure.

Based on the assumption that every applicant or candidate has met the basic formal educational standards, has taken the required number of courses, and read the necessary texts, the *PASSBOOK® SERIES* furnishes the one special preparation which may assure passing with confidence, instead of failing with insecurity. Examination questions – together with answers – are furnished as the basic vehicle for study so that the mysteries of the examination and its compounding difficulties may be eliminated or diminished by a sure method.

This book is meant to help you pass your examination provided that you qualify and are serious in your objective.

The entire field is reviewed through the huge store of content information which is succinctly presented through a provocative and challenging approach – the question-and-answer method.

A climate of success is established by furnishing the correct answers at the end of each test.

You soon learn to recognize types of questions, forms of questions, and patterns of questioning. You may even begin to anticipate expected outcomes.

You perceive that many questions are repeated or adapted so that you can gain acute insights, which may enable you to score many sure points.

You learn how to confront new questions, or types of questions, and to attack them confidently and work out the correct answers.

You note objectives and emphases, and recognize pitfalls and dangers, so that you may make positive educational adjustments.

Moreover, you are kept fully informed in relation to new concepts, methods, practices, and directions in the field.

You discover that you are actually taking the examination all the time: you are preparing for the examination by "taking" an examination, not by reading extraneous and/or supererogatory textbooks.

In short, this PASSBOOK®, used directedly, should be an important factor in helping you to pass your test.

CIVIL SERVICE SECRETARY

EXAMPLES OF WORK
Prepares correspondence, documents, records and other written material in final or draft form using handwritten, rough drafts, marked copy, oral records or data from various equipment as the source of material; Composes and prepares correspondence on matters where policies and procedures are well defined; Maintains and updates database/spreadsheet records on a personal computer; Screens callers or visitors to determine the nature of the inquiry and refers to appropriate party or office and answers inquiries as appropriate; Establishes and maintains confidential and general office files; Explains established program policies and procedures to the general public/clients and obtains routine information for program purposes; Receives, sorts and distributes incoming mail; Checks, codes and processes requisitions, claims and bills; Prepares and maintains financial, statistical and personnel records; Monitors and tracks status of program activities; Orders supplies and materials; Collects and gathers information to be used as a basis for reports and memoranda and prepares summaries; Transmits instructions from supervisor to staff and follows up to ensure deadlines are met; Supervises subordinate clerical personnel; Answers telephone and gives out information; May schedule conferences, meetings and make travel arrangements; Operates a personal computer, copier and other related peripheral office equipment.

SCOPE OF EXAMINATION
The written test will cover knowledge, skills, and/or abilities in such areas as:
1. Spelling;
2. Grammar, usage, punctuation;
3. Keyboarding practices;
4. Office recordkeeping; and
5. Office practices.

HOW TO TAKE A TEST

I. YOU MUST PASS AN EXAMINATION

A. WHAT EVERY CANDIDATE SHOULD KNOW

Examination applicants often ask us for help in preparing for the written test. What can I study in advance? What kinds of questions will be asked? How will the test be given? How will the papers be graded?

As an applicant for a civil service examination, you may be wondering about some of these things. Our purpose here is to suggest effective methods of advance study and to describe civil service examinations.

Your chances for success on this examination can be increased if you know how to prepare. Those "pre-examination jitters" can be reduced if you know what to expect. You can even experience an adventure in good citizenship if you know why civil service exams are given.

B. WHY ARE CIVIL SERVICE EXAMINATIONS GIVEN?

Civil service examinations are important to you in two ways. As a citizen, you want public jobs filled by employees who know how to do their work. As a job seeker, you want a fair chance to compete for that job on an equal footing with other candidates. The best-known means of accomplishing this two-fold goal is the competitive examination.

Exams are widely publicized throughout the nation. They may be administered for jobs in federal, state, city, municipal, town or village governments or agencies.

Any citizen may apply, with some limitations, such as the age or residence of applicants. Your experience and education may be reviewed to see whether you meet the requirements for the particular examination. When these requirements exist, they are reasonable and applied consistently to all applicants. Thus, a competitive examination may cause you some uneasiness now, but it is your privilege and safeguard.

C. HOW ARE CIVIL SERVICE EXAMS DEVELOPED?

Examinations are carefully written by trained technicians who are specialists in the field known as "psychological measurement," in consultation with recognized authorities in the field of work that the test will cover. These experts recommend the subject matter areas or skills to be tested; only those knowledges or skills important to your success on the job are included. The most reliable books and source materials available are used as references. Together, the experts and technicians judge the difficulty level of the questions.

Test technicians know how to phrase questions so that the problem is clearly stated. Their ethics do not permit "trick" or "catch" questions. Questions may have been tried out on sample groups, or subjected to statistical analysis, to determine their usefulness.

Written tests are often used in combination with performance tests, ratings of training and experience, and oral interviews. All of these measures combine to form the best-known means of finding the right person for the right job.

II. HOW TO PASS THE WRITTEN TEST

A. NATURE OF THE EXAMINATION

To prepare intelligently for civil service examinations, you should know how they differ from school examinations you have taken. In school you were assigned certain definite pages to read or subjects to cover. The examination questions were quite detailed and usually emphasized memory. Civil service exams, on the other hand, try to discover your present ability to perform the duties of a position, plus your potentiality to learn these duties. In other words, a civil service exam attempts to predict how successful you will be. Questions cover such a broad area that they cannot be as minute and detailed as school exam questions.

In the public service similar kinds of work, or positions, are grouped together in one "class." This process is known as *position-classification*. All the positions in a class are paid according to the salary range for that class. One class title covers all of these positions, and they are all tested by the same examination.

B. FOUR BASIC STEPS

1) Study the announcement

How, then, can you know what subjects to study? Our best answer is: "Learn as much as possible about the class of positions for which you've applied." The exam will test the knowledge, skills and abilities needed to do the work.

Your most valuable source of information about the position you want is the official exam announcement. This announcement lists the training and experience qualifications. Check these standards and apply only if you come reasonably close to meeting them.

The brief description of the position in the examination announcement offers some clues to the subjects which will be tested. Think about the job itself. Review the duties in your mind. Can you perform them, or are there some in which you are rusty? Fill in the blank spots in your preparation.

Many jurisdictions preview the written test in the exam announcement by including a section called "Knowledge and Abilities Required," "Scope of the Examination," or some similar heading. Here you will find out specifically what fields will be tested.

2) Review your own background

Once you learn in general what the position is all about, and what you need to know to do the work, ask yourself which subjects you already know fairly well and which need improvement. You may wonder whether to concentrate on improving your strong areas or on building some background in your fields of weakness. When the announcement has specified "some knowledge" or "considerable knowledge," or has used adjectives like "beginning principles of…" or "advanced … methods," you can get a clue as to the number and difficulty of questions to be asked in any given field. More questions, and hence broader coverage, would be included for those subjects which are more important in the work. Now weigh your strengths and weaknesses against the job requirements and prepare accordingly.

3) Determine the level of the position

Another way to tell how intensively you should prepare is to understand the level of the job for which you are applying. Is it the entering level? In other words, is this the position in which beginners in a field of work are hired? Or is it an intermediate or advanced level? Sometimes this is indicated by such words as "Junior" or "Senior" in the class title. Other jurisdictions use Roman numerals to designate the level – Clerk I, Clerk II, for example. The word "Supervisor" sometimes appears in the title. If the level is not indicated by the title, check the description of duties. Will you be working under very close supervision, or will you have responsibility for independent decisions in this work?

4) Choose appropriate study materials

Now that you know the subjects to be examined and the relative amount of each subject to be covered, you can choose suitable study materials. For beginning level jobs, or even advanced ones, if you have a pronounced weakness in some aspect of your training, read a modern, standard textbook in that field. Be sure it is up to date and has general coverage. Such books are normally available at your library, and the librarian will be glad to help you locate one. For entry-level positions, questions of appropriate difficulty are chosen – neither highly advanced questions, nor those too simple. Such questions require careful thought but not advanced training.

If the position for which you are applying is technical or advanced, you will read more advanced, specialized material. If you are already familiar with the basic principles of your field, elementary textbooks would waste your time. Concentrate on advanced textbooks and technical periodicals. Think through the concepts and review difficult problems in your field.

These are all general sources. You can get more ideas on your own initiative, following these leads. For example, training manuals and publications of the government agency which employs workers in your field can be useful, particularly for technical and professional positions. A letter or visit to the government department involved may result in more specific study suggestions, and certainly will provide you with a more definite idea of the exact nature of the position you are seeking.

III. KINDS OF TESTS

Tests are used for purposes other than measuring knowledge and ability to perform specified duties. For some positions, it is equally important to test ability to make adjustments to new situations or to profit from training. In others, basic mental abilities not dependent on information are essential. Questions which test these things may not appear as pertinent to the duties of the position as those which test for knowledge and information. Yet they are often highly important parts of a fair examination. For very general questions, it is almost impossible to help you direct your study efforts. What we can do is to point out some of the more common of these general abilities needed in public service positions and describe some typical questions.

1) General information

Broad, general information has been found useful for predicting job success in some kinds of work. This is tested in a variety of ways, from vocabulary lists to questions about current events. Basic background in some field of work, such as sociology or economics, may be sampled in a group of questions. Often these are principles which have become familiar to most persons through exposure rather than through formal training. It is difficult to advise you how to study for these questions; being alert to the world around you is our best suggestion.

2) Verbal ability

An example of an ability needed in many positions is verbal or language ability. Verbal ability is, in brief, the ability to use and understand words. Vocabulary and grammar tests are typical measures of this ability. Reading comprehension or paragraph interpretation questions are common in many kinds of civil service tests. You are given a paragraph of written material and asked to find its central meaning.

3) Numerical ability

Number skills can be tested by the familiar arithmetic problem, by checking paired lists of numbers to see which are alike and which are different, or by interpreting charts and graphs. In the latter test, a graph may be printed in the test booklet which you are asked to use as the basis for answering questions.

4) Observation

A popular test for law-enforcement positions is the observation test. A picture is shown to you for several minutes, then taken away. Questions about the picture test your ability to observe both details and larger elements.

5) Following directions

In many positions in the public service, the employee must be able to carry out written instructions dependably and accurately. You may be given a chart with several columns, each column listing a variety of information. The questions require you to carry out directions involving the information given in the chart.

6) Skills and aptitudes

Performance tests effectively measure some manual skills and aptitudes. When the skill is one in which you are trained, such as typing or shorthand, you can practice. These tests are often very much like those given in business school or high school courses. For many of the other skills and aptitudes, however, no short-time preparation can be made. Skills and abilities natural to you or that you have developed throughout your lifetime are being tested.

Many of the general questions just described provide all the data needed to answer the questions and ask you to use your reasoning ability to find the answers. Your best preparation for these tests, as well as for tests of facts and ideas, is to be at your physical and mental best. You, no doubt, have your own methods of getting into an exam-taking mood and keeping "in shape." The next section lists some ideas on this subject.

IV. KINDS OF QUESTIONS

Only rarely is the "essay" question, which you answer in narrative form, used in civil service tests. Civil service tests are usually of the short-answer type. Full instructions for answering these questions will be given to you at the examination. But in case this is your first experience with short-answer questions and separate answer sheets, here is what you need to know:

1) Multiple-choice Questions

Most popular of the short-answer questions is the "multiple choice" or "best answer" question. It can be used, for example, to test for factual knowledge, ability to solve problems or judgment in meeting situations found at work.

A multiple-choice question is normally one of three types—
- It can begin with an incomplete statement followed by several possible endings. You are to find the one ending which *best* completes the statement, although some of the others may not be entirely wrong.
- It can also be a complete statement in the form of a question which is answered by choosing one of the statements listed.

- It can be in the form of a problem – again you select the best answer.

Here is an example of a multiple-choice question with a discussion which should give you some clues as to the method for choosing the right answer:

When an employee has a complaint about his assignment, the action which will *best* help him overcome his difficulty is to
   A. discuss his difficulty with his coworkers
   B. take the problem to the head of the organization
   C. take the problem to the person who gave him the assignment
   D. say nothing to anyone about his complaint

In answering this question, you should study each of the choices to find which is best. Consider choice "A" – Certainly an employee may discuss his complaint with fellow employees, but no change or improvement can result, and the complaint remains unresolved. Choice "B" is a poor choice since the head of the organization probably does not know what assignment you have been given, and taking your problem to him is known as "going over the head" of the supervisor. The supervisor, or person who made the assignment, is the person who can clarify it or correct any injustice. Choice "C" is, therefore, correct. To say nothing, as in choice "D," is unwise. Supervisors have and interest in knowing the problems employees are facing, and the employee is seeking a solution to his problem.

2) True/False Questions

The "true/false" or "right/wrong" form of question is sometimes used. Here a complete statement is given. Your job is to decide whether the statement is right or wrong.

SAMPLE: A roaming cell-phone call to a nearby city costs less than a non-roaming call to a distant city.

This statement is wrong, or false, since roaming calls are more expensive.

This is not a complete list of all possible question forms, although most of the others are variations of these common types. You will always get complete directions for answering questions. Be sure you understand *how* to mark your answers – ask questions until you do.

V. RECORDING YOUR ANSWERS

Computer terminals are used more and more today for many different kinds of exams.

For an examination with very few applicants, you may be told to record your answers in the test booklet itself. Separate answer sheets are much more common. If this separate answer sheet is to be scored by machine – and this is often the case – it is highly important that you mark your answers correctly in order to get credit.

An electronic scoring machine is often used in civil service offices because of the speed with which papers can be scored. Machine-scored answer sheets must be marked with a pencil, which will be given to you. This pencil has a high graphite content which responds to the electronic scoring machine. As a matter of fact, stray dots may register as answers, so do not let your pencil rest on the answer sheet while you are pondering the correct answer. Also, if your pencil lead breaks or is otherwise defective, ask for another.

Since the answer sheet will be dropped in a slot in the scoring machine, be careful not to bend the corners or get the paper crumpled.

The answer sheet normally has five vertical columns of numbers, with 30 numbers to a column. These numbers correspond to the question numbers in your test booklet. After each number, going across the page are four or five pairs of dotted lines. These short dotted lines have small letters or numbers above them. The first two pairs may also have a "T" or "F" above the letters. This indicates that the first two pairs only are to be used if the questions are of the true-false type. If the questions are multiple choice, disregard the "T" and "F" and pay attention only to the small letters or numbers.

Answer your questions in the manner of the sample that follows:

32. The largest city in the United States is
    A. Washington, D.C.
    B. New York City
    C. Chicago
    D. Detroit
    E. San Francisco

1) Choose the answer you think is best. (New York City is the largest, so "B" is correct.)
2) Find the row of dotted lines numbered the same as the question you are answering. (Find row number 32)
3) Find the pair of dotted lines corresponding to the answer. (Find the pair of lines under the mark "B.")
4) Make a solid black mark between the dotted lines.

VI. BEFORE THE TEST

Common sense will help you find procedures to follow to get ready for an examination. Too many of us, however, overlook these sensible measures. Indeed, nervousness and fatigue have been found to be the most serious reasons why applicants fail to do their best on civil service tests. Here is a list of reminders:

- Begin your preparation early – Don't wait until the last minute to go scurrying around for books and materials or to find out what the position is all about.
- Prepare continuously – An hour a night for a week is better than an all-night cram session. This has been definitely established. What is more, a night a week for a month will return better dividends than crowding your study into a shorter period of time.
- Locate the place of the exam – You have been sent a notice telling you when and where to report for the examination. If the location is in a different town or otherwise unfamiliar to you, it would be well to inquire the best route and learn something about the building.
- Relax the night before the test – Allow your mind to rest. Do not study at all that night. Plan some mild recreation or diversion; then go to bed early and get a good night's sleep.
- Get up early enough to make a leisurely trip to the place for the test – This way unforeseen events, traffic snarls, unfamiliar buildings, etc. will not upset you.
- Dress comfortably – A written test is not a fashion show. You will be known by number and not by name, so wear something comfortable.

- Leave excess paraphernalia at home – Shopping bags and odd bundles will get in your way. You need bring only the items mentioned in the official notice you received; usually everything you need is provided. Do not bring reference books to the exam. They will only confuse those last minutes and be taken away from you when in the test room.
- Arrive somewhat ahead of time – If because of transportation schedules you must get there very early, bring a newspaper or magazine to take your mind off yourself while waiting.
- Locate the examination room – When you have found the proper room, you will be directed to the seat or part of the room where you will sit. Sometimes you are given a sheet of instructions to read while you are waiting. Do not fill out any forms until you are told to do so; just read them and be prepared.
- Relax and prepare to listen to the instructions
- If you have any physical problem that may keep you from doing your best, be sure to tell the test administrator. If you are sick or in poor health, you really cannot do your best on the exam. You can come back and take the test some other time.

VII. AT THE TEST

The day of the test is here and you have the test booklet in your hand. The temptation to get going is very strong. Caution! There is more to success than knowing the right answers. You must know how to identify your papers and understand variations in the type of short-answer question used in this particular examination. Follow these suggestions for maximum results from your efforts:

1) Cooperate with the monitor

The test administrator has a duty to create a situation in which you can be as much at ease as possible. He will give instructions, tell you when to begin, check to see that you are marking your answer sheet correctly, and so on. He is not there to guard you, although he will see that your competitors do not take unfair advantage. He wants to help you do your best.

2) Listen to all instructions

Don't jump the gun! Wait until you understand all directions. In most civil service tests you get more time than you need to answer the questions. So don't be in a hurry. Read each word of instructions until you clearly understand the meaning. Study the examples, listen to all announcements and follow directions. Ask questions if you do not understand what to do.

3) Identify your papers

Civil service exams are usually identified by number only. You will be assigned a number; you must not put your name on your test papers. Be sure to copy your number correctly. Since more than one exam may be given, copy your exact examination title.

4) Plan your time

Unless you are told that a test is a "speed" or "rate of work" test, speed itself is usually not important. Time enough to answer all the questions will be provided, but this does not mean that you have all day. An overall time limit has been set. Divide the total time (in minutes) by the number of questions to determine the approximate time you have for each question.

5) Do not linger over difficult questions

If you come across a difficult question, mark it with a paper clip (useful to have along) and come back to it when you have been through the booklet. One caution if you do this – be sure to skip a number on your answer sheet as well. Check often to be sure that you have not lost your place and that you are marking in the row numbered the same as the question you are answering.

6) Read the questions

Be sure you know what the question asks! Many capable people are unsuccessful because they failed to *read* the questions correctly.

7) Answer all questions

Unless you have been instructed that a penalty will be deducted for incorrect answers, it is better to guess than to omit a question.

8) Speed tests

It is often better NOT to guess on speed tests. It has been found that on timed tests people are tempted to spend the last few seconds before time is called in marking answers at random – without even reading them – in the hope of picking up a few extra points. To discourage this practice, the instructions may warn you that your score will be "corrected" for guessing. That is, a penalty will be applied. The incorrect answers will be deducted from the correct ones, or some other penalty formula will be used.

9) Review your answers

If you finish before time is called, go back to the questions you guessed or omitted to give them further thought. Review other answers if you have time.

10) Return your test materials

If you are ready to leave before others have finished or time is called, take ALL your materials to the monitor and leave quietly. Never take any test material with you. The monitor can discover whose papers are not complete, and taking a test booklet may be grounds for disqualification.

VIII. EXAMINATION TECHNIQUES

1) Read the general instructions carefully. These are usually printed on the first page of the exam booklet. As a rule, these instructions refer to the timing of the examination; the fact that you should not start work until the signal and must stop work at a signal, etc. If there are any *special* instructions, such as a choice of questions to be answered, make sure that you note this instruction carefully.

2) When you are ready to start work on the examination, that is as soon as the signal has been given, read the instructions to each question booklet, underline any key words or phrases, such as *least, best, outline, describe* and the like. In this way you will tend to answer as requested rather than discover on reviewing your paper that you *listed without describing*, that you selected the *worst* choice rather than the *best* choice, etc.

3) If the examination is of the objective or multiple-choice type – that is, each question will also give a series of possible answers: A, B, C or D, and you are called upon to select the best answer and write the letter next to that answer on your answer paper – it is advisable to start answering each question in turn. There may be anywhere from 50 to 100 such questions in the three or four hours allotted and you can see how much time would be taken if you read through all the questions before beginning to answer any. Furthermore, if you come across a question or group of questions which you know would be difficult to answer, it would undoubtedly affect your handling of all the other questions.

4) If the examination is of the essay type and contains but a few questions, it is a moot point as to whether you should read all the questions before starting to answer any one. Of course, if you are given a choice – say five out of seven and the like – then it is essential to read all the questions so you can eliminate the two that are most difficult. If, however, you are asked to answer all the questions, there may be danger in trying to answer the easiest one first because you may find that you will spend too much time on it. The best technique is to answer the first question, then proceed to the second, etc.

5) Time your answers. Before the exam begins, write down the time it started, then add the time allowed for the examination and write down the time it must be completed, then divide the time available somewhat as follows:
   - If 3-1/2 hours are allowed, that would be 210 minutes. If you have 80 objective-type questions, that would be an average of 2-1/2 minutes per question. Allow yourself no more than 2 minutes per question, or a total of 160 minutes, which will permit about 50 minutes to review.
   - If for the time allotment of 210 minutes there are 7 essay questions to answer, that would average about 30 minutes a question. Give yourself only 25 minutes per question so that you have about 35 minutes to review.

6) The most important instruction is to *read each question* and make sure you know what is wanted. The second most important instruction is to *time yourself properly* so that you answer every question. The third most important instruction is to *answer every question*. Guess if you have to but include something for each question. Remember that you will receive no credit for a blank and will probably receive some credit if you write something in answer to an essay question. If you guess a letter – say "B" for a multiple-choice question – you may have guessed right. If you leave a blank as an answer to a multiple-choice question, the examiners may respect your feelings but it will not add a point to your score. Some exams may penalize you for wrong answers, so in such cases *only*, you may not want to guess unless you have some basis for your answer.

7) Suggestions
   a. Objective-type questions
      1. Examine the question booklet for proper sequence of pages and questions
      2. Read all instructions carefully
      3. Skip any question which seems too difficult; return to it after all other questions have been answered
      4. Apportion your time properly; do not spend too much time on any single question or group of questions

5. Note and underline key words – *all, most, fewest, least, best, worst, same, opposite,* etc.
6. Pay particular attention to negatives
7. Note unusual option, e.g., unduly long, short, complex, different or similar in content to the body of the question
8. Observe the use of "hedging" words – *probably, may, most likely,* etc.
9. Make sure that your answer is put next to the same number as the question
10. Do not second-guess unless you have good reason to believe the second answer is definitely more correct
11. Cross out original answer if you decide another answer is more accurate; do not erase until you are ready to hand your paper in
12. Answer all questions; guess unless instructed otherwise
13. Leave time for review

b. Essay questions
1. Read each question carefully
2. Determine exactly what is wanted. Underline key words or phrases.
3. Decide on outline or paragraph answer
4. Include many different points and elements unless asked to develop any one or two points or elements
5. Show impartiality by giving pros and cons unless directed to select one side only
6. Make and write down any assumptions you find necessary to answer the questions
7. Watch your English, grammar, punctuation and choice of words
8. Time your answers; don't crowd material

8) Answering the essay question

Most essay questions can be answered by framing the specific response around several key words or ideas. Here are a few such key words or ideas:

M's: manpower, materials, methods, money, management
P's: purpose, program, policy, plan, procedure, practice, problems, pitfalls, personnel, public relations

a. Six basic steps in handling problems:
1. Preliminary plan and background development
2. Collect information, data and facts
3. Analyze and interpret information, data and facts
4. Analyze and develop solutions as well as make recommendations
5. Prepare report and sell recommendations
6. Install recommendations and follow up effectiveness

b. Pitfalls to avoid
1. *Taking things for granted* – A statement of the situation does not necessarily imply that each of the elements is necessarily true; for example, a complaint may be invalid and biased so that all that can be taken for granted is that a complaint has been registered

2. *Considering only one side of a situation* – Wherever possible, indicate several alternatives and then point out the reasons you selected the best one
3. *Failing to indicate follow up* – Whenever your answer indicates action on your part, make certain that you will take proper follow-up action to see how successful your recommendations, procedures or actions turn out to be
4. *Taking too long in answering any single question* – Remember to time your answers properly

IX. AFTER THE TEST

Scoring procedures differ in detail among civil service jurisdictions although the general principles are the same. Whether the papers are hand-scored or graded by machine we have described, they are nearly always graded by number. That is, the person who marks the paper knows only the number – never the name – of the applicant. Not until all the papers have been graded will they be matched with names. If other tests, such as training and experience or oral interview ratings have been given, scores will be combined. Different parts of the examination usually have different weights. For example, the written test might count 60 percent of the final grade, and a rating of training and experience 40 percent. In many jurisdictions, veterans will have a certain number of points added to their grades.

After the final grade has been determined, the names are placed in grade order and an eligible list is established. There are various methods for resolving ties between those who get the same final grade – probably the most common is to place first the name of the person whose application was received first. Job offers are made from the eligible list in the order the names appear on it. You will be notified of your grade and your rank as soon as all these computations have been made. This will be done as rapidly as possible.

People who are found to meet the requirements in the announcement are called "eligibles." Their names are put on a list of eligible candidates. An eligible's chances of getting a job depend on how high he stands on this list and how fast agencies are filling jobs from the list.

When a job is to be filled from a list of eligibles, the agency asks for the names of people on the list of eligibles for that job. When the civil service commission receives this request, it sends to the agency the names of the three people highest on this list. Or, if the job to be filled has specialized requirements, the office sends the agency the names of the top three persons who meet these requirements from the general list.

The appointing officer makes a choice from among the three people whose names were sent to him. If the selected person accepts the appointment, the names of the others are put back on the list to be considered for future openings.

That is the rule in hiring from all kinds of eligible lists, whether they are for typist, carpenter, chemist, or something else. For every vacancy, the appointing officer has his choice of any one of the top three eligibles on the list. This explains why the person whose name is on top of the list sometimes does not get an appointment when some of the persons lower on the list do. If the appointing officer chooses the second or third eligible, the No. 1 eligible does not get a job at once, but stays on the list until he is appointed or the list is terminated.

X. HOW TO PASS THE INTERVIEW TEST

The examination for which you applied requires an oral interview test. You have already taken the written test and you are now being called for the interview test – the final part of the formal examination.

You may think that it is not possible to prepare for an interview test and that there are no procedures to follow during an interview. Our purpose is to point out some things you can do in advance that will help you and some good rules to follow and pitfalls to avoid while you are being interviewed.

What is an interview supposed to test?

The written examination is designed to test the technical knowledge and competence of the candidate; the oral is designed to evaluate intangible qualities, not readily measured otherwise, and to establish a list showing the relative fitness of each candidate – as measured against his competitors – for the position sought. Scoring is not on the basis of "right" and "wrong," but on a sliding scale of values ranging from "not passable" to "outstanding." As a matter of fact, it is possible to achieve a relatively low score without a single "incorrect" answer because of evident weakness in the qualities being measured.

Occasionally, an examination may consist entirely of an oral test – either an individual or a group oral. In such cases, information is sought concerning the technical knowledges and abilities of the candidate, since there has been no written examination for this purpose. More commonly, however, an oral test is used to supplement a written examination.

Who conducts interviews?

The composition of oral boards varies among different jurisdictions. In nearly all, a representative of the personnel department serves as chairman. One of the members of the board may be a representative of the department in which the candidate would work. In some cases, "outside experts" are used, and, frequently, a businessman or some other representative of the general public is asked to serve. Labor and management or other special groups may be represented. The aim is to secure the services of experts in the appropriate field.

However the board is composed, it is a good idea (and not at all improper or unethical) to ascertain in advance of the interview who the members are and what groups they represent. When you are introduced to them, you will have some idea of their backgrounds and interests, and at least you will not stutter and stammer over their names.

What should be done before the interview?

While knowledge about the board members is useful and takes some of the surprise element out of the interview, there is other preparation which is more substantive. It *is* possible to prepare for an oral interview – in several ways:

1) Keep a copy of your application and review it carefully before the interview

This may be the only document before the oral board, and the starting point of the interview. Know what education and experience you have listed there, and the sequence and dates of all of it. Sometimes the board will ask you to review the highlights of your experience for them; you should not have to hem and haw doing it.

2) Study the class specification and the examination announcement

Usually, the oral board has one or both of these to guide them. The qualities, characteristics or knowledges required by the position sought are stated in these documents. They offer valuable clues as to the nature of the oral interview. For example, if the job involves supervisory responsibilities, the announcement will usually indicate that knowledge of modern supervisory methods and the qualifications of the candidate as a supervisor will be tested. If so, you can expect such questions, frequently in the form of a hypothetical situation which you are expected to solve. NEVER go into an oral without knowledge of the duties and responsibilities of the job you seek.

3) Think through each qualification required

Try to visualize the kind of questions you would ask if you were a board member. How well could you answer them? Try especially to appraise your own knowledge and background in each area, *measured against the job sought*, and identify any areas in which you are weak. Be critical and realistic – do not flatter yourself.

4) Do some general reading in areas in which you feel you may be weak

For example, if the job involves supervision and your past experience has NOT, some general reading in supervisory methods and practices, particularly in the field of human relations, might be useful. Do NOT study agency procedures or detailed manuals. The oral board will be testing your understanding and capacity, not your memory.

5) Get a good night's sleep and watch your general health and mental attitude

You will want a clear head at the interview. Take care of a cold or any other minor ailment, and of course, no hangovers.

What should be done on the day of the interview?

Now comes the day of the interview itself. Give yourself plenty of time to get there. Plan to arrive somewhat ahead of the scheduled time, particularly if your appointment is in the fore part of the day. If a previous candidate fails to appear, the board might be ready for you a bit early. By early afternoon an oral board is almost invariably behind schedule if there are many candidates, and you may have to wait. Take along a book or magazine to read, or your application to review, but leave any extraneous material in the waiting room when you go in for your interview. In any event, relax and compose yourself.

The matter of dress is important. The board is forming impressions about you – from your experience, your manners, your attitude, and your appearance. Give your personal appearance careful attention. Dress your best, but not your flashiest. Choose conservative, appropriate clothing, and be sure it is immaculate. This is a business interview, and your appearance should indicate that you regard it as such. Besides, being well groomed and properly dressed will help boost your confidence.

Sooner or later, someone will call your name and escort you into the interview room. *This is it.* From here on you are on your own. It is too late for any more preparation. But remember, you asked for this opportunity to prove your fitness, and you are here because your request was granted.

What happens when you go in?

The usual sequence of events will be as follows: The clerk (who is often the board stenographer) will introduce you to the chairman of the oral board, who will introduce you to the other members of the board. Acknowledge the introductions before you sit down. Do not be surprised if you find a microphone facing you or a stenotypist sitting by. Oral interviews are usually recorded in the event of an appeal or other review.

Usually the chairman of the board will open the interview by reviewing the highlights of your education and work experience from your application – primarily for the benefit of the other members of the board, as well as to get the material into the record. Do not interrupt or comment unless there is an error or significant misinterpretation; if that is the case, do not hesitate. But do not quibble about insignificant matters. Also, he will usually ask you some question about your education, experience or your present job – partly to get you to start talking and to establish the interviewing "rapport." He may start the actual questioning, or turn it over to one of the other members. Frequently, each member undertakes the questioning on a particular area, one in which he is perhaps most competent, so you can expect each member to participate in the examination. Because time is limited, you may also expect some rather abrupt switches in the direction the questioning takes, so do not be upset by it. Normally, a board member will not pursue a single line of questioning unless he discovers a particular strength or weakness.

After each member has participated, the chairman will usually ask whether any member has any further questions, then will ask you if you have anything you wish to add. Unless you are expecting this question, it may floor you. Worse, it may start you off on an extended, extemporaneous speech. The board is not usually seeking more information. The question is principally to offer you a last opportunity to present further qualifications or to indicate that you have nothing to add. So, if you feel that a significant qualification or characteristic has been overlooked, it is proper to point it out in a sentence or so. Do not compliment the board on the thoroughness of their examination – they have been sketchy, and you know it. If you wish, merely say, "No thank you, I have nothing further to add." This is a point where you can "talk yourself out" of a good impression or fail to present an important bit of information. Remember, *you close the interview yourself.*

The chairman will then say, "That is all, Mr. _____, thank you." Do not be startled; the interview is over, and quicker than you think. Thank him, gather your belongings and take your leave. Save your sigh of relief for the other side of the door.

How to put your best foot forward

Throughout this entire process, you may feel that the board individually and collectively is trying to pierce your defenses, seek out your hidden weaknesses and embarrass and confuse you. Actually, this is not true. They are obliged to make an appraisal of your qualifications for the job you are seeking, and they want to see you in your best light. Remember, they must interview all candidates and a non-cooperative candidate may become a failure in spite of their best efforts to bring out his qualifications. Here are 15 suggestions that will help you:

1) Be natural – Keep your attitude confident, not cocky

If you are not confident that you can do the job, do not expect the board to be. Do not apologize for your weaknesses, try to bring out your strong points. The board is interested in a positive, not negative, presentation. Cockiness will antagonize any board member and make him wonder if you are covering up a weakness by a false show of strength.

2) Get comfortable, but don't lounge or sprawl

Sit erectly but not stiffly. A careless posture may lead the board to conclude that you are careless in other things, or at least that you are not impressed by the importance of the occasion. Either conclusion is natural, even if incorrect. Do not fuss with your clothing, a pencil or an ashtray. Your hands may occasionally be useful to emphasize a point; do not let them become a point of distraction.

3) Do not wisecrack or make small talk

This is a serious situation, and your attitude should show that you consider it as such. Further, the time of the board is limited – they do not want to waste it, and neither should you.

4) Do not exaggerate your experience or abilities

In the first place, from information in the application or other interviews and sources, the board may know more about you than you think. Secondly, you probably will not get away with it. An experienced board is rather adept at spotting such a situation, so do not take the chance.

5) If you know a board member, do not make a point of it, yet do not hide it

Certainly you are not fooling him, and probably not the other members of the board. Do not try to take advantage of your acquaintanceship – it will probably do you little good.

6) Do not dominate the interview

Let the board do that. They will give you the clues – do not assume that you have to do all the talking. Realize that the board has a number of questions to ask you, and do not try to take up all the interview time by showing off your extensive knowledge of the answer to the first one.

7) Be attentive

You only have 20 minutes or so, and you should keep your attention at its sharpest throughout. When a member is addressing a problem or question to you, give him your undivided attention. Address your reply principally to him, but do not exclude the other board members.

8) Do not interrupt

A board member may be stating a problem for you to analyze. He will ask you a question when the time comes. Let him state the problem, and wait for the question.

9) Make sure you understand the question

Do not try to answer until you are sure what the question is. If it is not clear, restate it in your own words or ask the board member to clarify it for you. However, do not haggle about minor elements.

10) Reply promptly but not hastily

A common entry on oral board rating sheets is "candidate responded readily," or "candidate hesitated in replies." Respond as promptly and quickly as you can, but do not jump to a hasty, ill-considered answer.

11) Do not be peremptory in your answers

A brief answer is proper – but do not fire your answer back. That is a losing game from your point of view. The board member can probably ask questions much faster than you can answer them.

12) Do not try to create the answer you think the board member wants

He is interested in what kind of mind you have and how it works – not in playing games. Furthermore, he can usually spot this practice and will actually grade you down on it.

13) Do not switch sides in your reply merely to agree with a board member

Frequently, a member will take a contrary position merely to draw you out and to see if you are willing and able to defend your point of view. Do not start a debate, yet do not surrender a good position. If a position is worth taking, it is worth defending.

14) Do not be afraid to admit an error in judgment if you are shown to be wrong

The board knows that you are forced to reply without any opportunity for careful consideration. Your answer may be demonstrably wrong. If so, admit it and get on with the interview.

15) Do not dwell at length on your present job

The opening question may relate to your present assignment. Answer the question but do not go into an extended discussion. You are being examined for a *new* job, not your present one. As a matter of fact, try to phrase ALL your answers in terms of the job for which you are being examined.

Basis of Rating

Probably you will forget most of these "do's" and "don'ts" when you walk into the oral interview room. Even remembering them all will not ensure you a passing grade. Perhaps you did not have the qualifications in the first place. But remembering them will help you to put your best foot forward, without treading on the toes of the board members.

Rumor and popular opinion to the contrary notwithstanding, an oral board wants you to make the best appearance possible. They know you are under pressure – but they also want to see how you respond to it as a guide to what your reaction would be under the pressures of the job you seek. They will be influenced by the degree of poise you display, the personal traits you show and the manner in which you respond.

ABOUT THIS BOOK

This book contains tests divided into Examination Sections. Go through each test, answering every question in the margin. We have also attached a sample answer sheet at the back of the book that can be removed and used. At the end of each test look at the answer key and check your answers. On the ones you got wrong, look at the right answer choice and learn. Do not fill in the answers first. Do not memorize the questions and answers, but understand the answer and principles involved. On your test, the questions will likely be different from the samples. Questions are changed and new ones added. If you understand these past questions you should have success with any changes that arise. Tests may consist of several types of questions. We have additional books on each subject should more study be advisable or necessary for you. Finally, the more you study, the better prepared you will be. This book is intended to be the last thing you study before you walk into the examination room. Prior study of relevant texts is also recommended. NLC publishes some of these in our Fundamental Series. Knowledge and good sense are important factors in passing your exam. Good luck also helps. So now study this Passbook, absorb the material contained within and take that knowledge into the examination. Then do your best to pass that exam.

EXAMINATION SECTION

EXAMINATION SECTION

TEST 1

DIRECTIONS: Each question or incomplete statement is followed by several suggested answers or completions. Select the one that BEST answers the question or completes the statement. *PRINT THE LETTER OF THE CORRECT ANSWER IN THE SPACE AT THE RIGHT.*

1. The one of the following that is MOST advisable to do before transcribing your dictation notes is to
    A. check the syllabification of long words for typing purposes
    B. edit your notes
    C. number the pages of dictation
    D. sort them by the kind of typing format required

    1._____

2. As a secretary, the one of the following which is LEAST important in writing a letter under your own signature is
    A. the accuracy of the information
    B. the appropriateness of the language
    C. the reason for the letter
    D. your supervisor's approval of the final copy

    2._____

3. In a typed letter, the reference line is used
    A. for identification purposes on typed pages of more than one page
    B. to indicate under what heading the copy of the letter should be filed
    C. to indicate who dictated the letter and who typed it
    D. to make the subject of the letter prominent by typing it a single space below the salutation

    3._____

Questions 4-5:

DIRECTIONS: For questions 4 and 5, choose the letter of the sentence that BEST and MOST clearly expresses its meaning.

4. A. It has always been the practice of this office to effectuate recruitment of prospective employees from other departments.
    B. This office has always made a practice of recruiting prospective employees from other departments.
    C. Recruitment of prospective employees from other departments has always been a practice which has been implemented by this office.
    D. Implementation of the policy of recruitment of prospective employees from other departments has always been a practice of this office.

    4._____

5. A. These employees are assigned to the level of work evidenced by their efforts and skills during the training period.
   B. The level of work to which these employees is assigned is decided upon on the basis of the efforts and skills evidenced by them during the period in which they were trained.
   C. Assignment of these employees is made on the basis of the level of work their efforts and skills during the training period has evidenced.
   D. These employees are assigned to a level of work their efforts and skills during the training period have evidenced.

5._____

6. An office assistant was asked to mail a duplicated report of 100 pages to a professor in an out-of-town university. The professor sending the report dictated a short letter that he wanted to mail with the report.
   Of the following, the MOST inexpensive proper means of sending these two items would be to send the report
   A. and the letter first class
   B. by parcel post and the letter separately by air mail
   C. and the letter by parcel post
   D. by parcel post and attach to the package an envelope with first-class postage in which is enclosed the letter

6._____

7. Plans are underway to determine the productivity of the typists who work in a central office. Of the procedures listed, the one generally considered the MOST accurate for finding out the typists' output is to
   A. keep a record of how much typing is done over specified periods of time
   B. ask each typist how fast she types when she is doing a great deal of word processing
   C. give each typist a timed test during a specified period
   D. ask the supervisor to estimate the typing speed of each subordinate

7._____

8. Assume that an executive regularly receives the four types of mail listed below.
   As a general rule, the executive's secretary should arrange the mail from top to bottom so that the top items are
   A. advertisements
   B. airmail letters
   C. business letters
   D. unopened personal letters

8._____

9. An office assistant in transcribing reports and letters from dictation should MOST generally assume that
    A. the transcript should be exactly what was dictated so there is little need to check any details
    B. the dictated material is merely an idea of what the dictator wanted to say so changes should be made to improve any part of the dictation
    C. there may be some slight changes, but essentially the transcription is to be a faithful copy of what was dictated
    D. the transcript is merely a very rough draft and should be typed quickly so that the dictator can review it and make changes preliminary to having the final copy typed

9._____

10. The one of the following which generally is the CHIEF disadvantage of using office machines in place of human workers in office work is that the machines are
    A. slower
    B. less accurate
    C. more costly
    D. less flexible

10._____

11. An office assistant in a New York City college is asked to place a call to a prospective visiting professor in Los Angeles. It is 1 p.m. in New York (EST). The time in Los Angeles is
    A. 9 a.m.   B. 10 a.m.   C. 4 p.m.   D. 5 p.m.

11._____

12. An office assistant is instructed to send a copy of a report to a professor located in a building across campus. The fastest and most efficient way for this report to reach the professor is by
    A. sending a messenger to hand-deliver it to the professor's office
    B. sending it via fax to the main office of the professor's department
    C. e-mailing it to the professor
    D. dictating the contents of the report to the professor over the phone

12._____

13. An office assistant is in the process of typing the forms for recommendation for promotion for a member of the faculty who is away for a week. She notes that two books of which he is the author are listed without dates.
    Of the following, the procedure she should BEST follow at this point generally is to
    A. postpone doing the job until the professor returns to campus the following week
    B. type the material omitting the books
    C. check the professor's office for copies of the books and obtain the correct data
    D. call the professor's wife and ask her when the books were published

13._____

14. An office has introduced work standards for all of the employees.
Of the following, it is MOST likely that use of such standards would tend to
    A. make it more difficult to determine numbers of employees needed
    B. lead to a substantial drop in morale among all of the employees
    C. reduce the possibility of planning to meet emergencies
    D. reduce uncertainty about the costs of doing tasks

15. Of the following clerical errors, the one which probably is LEAST important is
    A. adding 543 instead of 548 to a bookkeeping account
    B. putting the wrong code on a data processing card
    C. recording a transaction on the record of Henry Smith instead of on the record of Harry Smith
    D. writing John Murpfy instead of John Murphy when addressing an envelope

16. Of the following errors, the one which probably is MOST important is
    A. writing "they're" instead of "their" in an office memo
    B. misplacing a decimal point on a sales invoice
    C. forgetting to write the date on a note for a supervisor
    D. sending an e-mail to a misspelled e-mail address

17. The chairman of an academic department tells an office assistant that a meeting of the faculty is to be held four weeks from the current date.
Of the following responsibilities, the office assistant is MOST frequently held responsible for
    A. planning the agenda of the meeting
    B. presiding over the conduct of the meeting
    C. reserving the meeting room and notifying the members
    D. initiating all formal resolutions

18. Of the following, a centralized filing system is LEAST suitable for filing
    A. material which is confidential in nature
    B. routine correspondence
    C. periodic reports of the divisions of the department
    D. material used by several divisions of the department

19. A misplaced record is a lost record.
Of the following, the MOST valid implication of this statement in regard to office work is that
    A. all records in an office should be filed in strict alphabetical order
    B. accuracy in filing is essential
    C. only one method of filing should be used throughout the office
    D. files should be locked when not in use

20. When typing names or titles on a roll of folder labels, the one of the following which is MOST important to do is to type the caption
    A. as it appears on the papers to be placed in the folder
    B. in capital letters
    C. in exact indexing or filing order
    D. so that it appears near the bottom of the folder tab when the label is attached

20._____

21. A professor at a Boston university asks an office assistant to place a call to a fellow professor in San Francisco. The MOST appropriate local time for the assistant to place the call to the professor in California, given the time difference, would be
    A. 8:30 a.m.   B. 10:00 a.m.   C. 11:30 a.m.   D. 1:30 p.m.

21._____

22. When typing the rough draft of a report, the computer application you would use is
    A. Excel   B. Word
    C. PowerPoint   D. Internet Explorer

22._____

23. Which of the following is the BEST and most appropriate way to proofread and edit a report before submitting it to a supervisor for review?
    A. Scan the report with the program's spell check feature
    B. Proof the report yourself, then ask another office assistant to read the report over as well until it is finished
    C. Give the report to another office assistant who is more skilled at proofreading
    D. Use the spell checker, then scan the report yourself as many times as needed in order to pick up any additional errors

23._____

24. The one of the following situations in which it would be MOST justifiable for an office to use standard or form paragraphs in its business letters is when
    A. a large number of similar letters is to be sent
    B. the letters are to be uniform in length and appearance
    C. it is desired to reduce typing errors in correspondence
    D. the office is to carry on a lengthy correspondence with an individual

24._____

25. Of the following, the MOST important factor in determining whether or not an office filing system is effective is that the
    A. information in the files is legible
    B. records in the files are used frequently
    C. information in the files is accurate
    D. records in the files can be located readily

25._____

KEY (CORRECT ANSWERS)

1. B	11. B	21. D
2. D	12. C	22. B
3. C	13. C	23. D
4. B	14. D	24. A
5. A	15. D	25. D
6. D	16. B	
7. A	17. C	
8. D	18. A	
9. C	19. B	
10. D	20. C	

TEST 2

DIRECTIONS: Each question or incomplete statement is followed by several suggested answers or completions. Select the one that BEST answers the question or completes the statement. *PRINT THE LETTER OF THE CORRECT ANSWER IN THE SPACE AT THE RIGHT.*

1. For the office assistant whose duties include frequent recording and transcription of minutes of formal meetings, the one of the following reference works generally considered to be MOST useful is
    A. *Robert's Rules of Order*
    B. *Bartlett's Familiar Quotations*
    C. *World Almanac and Book of Facts*
    D. *Conway's Reference*

    1._____

2. Of the following statements about the numeric system of filing, the one which is CORRECT is that it
    A. is the least accurate of all methods of filing
    B. eliminates the need for cross-referencing
    C. allows for very limited expansion
    D. requires a separate index

    2._____

3. When more than one name or subject is involved in a piece of correspondence to be filed, the office assistant should GENERALLY
    A. prepare a cross-reference sheet
    B. establish a geographical filing system
    C. prepare out-guides
    D. establish a separate index card file for noting such correspondence

    3._____

4. A tickler file is MOST generally used for
    A. identification of material contained in a numeric file
    B. maintenance of a current listing of telephone numbers
    C. follow-up of matters requiring future attention
    D. control of records borrowed or otherwise removed from the files

    4._____

5. In filing, the name Ms. *Ann Catalana-Moss* should GENERALLY be indexed as
    A. Moss, Catalana, Ann (Ms.)
    B. Catalana-Moss, Ann (Ms.)
    C. Ann Catalana-Moss (Ms.)
    D. Moss-Catalana, Ann (Ms.)

    5._____

6. An office assistant has a set of four cards, each of which contains one of the following names.
   In alphabetic filing, the FIRST of the cards to be filed is
   A. Ms. Alma John
   B. Mrs. John (Patricia) Edwards
   C. John-Edward School Supplies, Inc.
   D. John H. Edwards

6._____

7. Generally, of the following, the name to be filed FIRST in an alphabetical filing system is
   A. Diane Maestro
   B. Diana McElroy
   C. James Mackell
   D. James McKell

7._____

8. After checking several times, you are unable to locate a student record in its proper file drawer. The file drawer in question is used constantly by many members of the staff.
   In this situation, the NEXT step you should take in locating the missing record is to
   A. ask another worker to look through the file drawer
   B. determine if there is another copy of the record filed in a different place
   C. find out if the record has been removed by another staff member
   D. wait a day or two and see if the record turns up

8._____

9. It is MOST important that an enclosure which is to be mailed with a letter should be put in an envelope so that
   A. any printing on the enclosure will not be visible through the address side of the envelope
   B. it is obvious that there is an enclosure inside the envelope
   C. the enclosure takes up less space than the letter
   D. the person who opens the envelope will pull out both the letter and the enclosure

9._____

10. Suppose that one of the student aides with whom you work suggests a change in the filing procedure. He is sure the change will result in increased rates of filing among the other employees.
    The one of the following which you should do FIRST is to
    A. ask him to demonstrate his method in order to determine if he files more quickly than the other employees
    B. ask your supervisor if you may make a change in the filing procedure
    C. ignore the aide's suggestion since he is not a filing expert
    D. tell him to show his method to the other employees and to encourage them to use it

10._____

11. It is generally advisable to leave at least six inches of working space in a file drawer. This procedure is MOST useful in
    A. decreasing the number of filing errors
    B. facilitating the sorting of documents and folders
    C. maintaining a regular program of removing inactive records
    D. preventing folders and papers from being torn

11._____

12. Assume that a dictator is briefly interrupted because of a telephone call or other similar matter (no more than three minutes).
Of the following tasks, the person taking the dictation should NORMALLY use the time to
    A. re-read notes already recorded
    B. tidy the dictator's desk
    C. check the accuracy of the dictator's desk files
    D. return to her own desk to type the dictated material

12._____

13. When typing a preliminary draft of a report, the one of the following which you should generally NOT do is
    A. erase typing errors and deletions rather than cross them out
    B. leave plenty of room at the top, bottom and sides of each page
    C. make only the number of copies that you are asked to make
    D. type double or triple space

13._____

14. The BEST way for a receptionist to deal with a situation in which she must leave her desk for a long time is to
    A. ask someone to take her place while she is away
    B. leave a note or sign on her desk which indicates the time she will return
    C. take a chance that no one will arrive while she is gone and leave her desk unattended
    D. tell a coworker to ask any visitors that arrive to wait until she returns

14._____

15. Suppose that two individuals come up to your desk at the same time. One of them asks you for the location of the nearest public phone. After you answer the question, you turn to the second person who asks you the same question.
The one of the following actions that would be BEST for you to take in this situation is to
    A. ignore the second person since he obviously overheard your first answer
    B. point out that you just answered the same question and quickly repeat the information
    C. politely repeat the information to the second individual
    D. tell the second person to follow the first to the public telephone

15._____

16. Which of the following names should be filed FIRST in an alphabetical filing system? 16._____
    A. Anthony Aarvedsen   B. William Aaron
    C. Denise Aron   D. A.J. Arrington

17. New material added to a file folder should USUALLY be inserted 17._____
    A. in the order of importance (the most important in front)
    B. in the order of importance (the most important in back)
    C. chronologically (most recent in front)
    D. chronologically (most recent in back)

18. An individual is looking for a name in the White Pages of a telephone directory. 18._____
    Which of the following BEST describes the system of filing found there?
    A. alphabetic   B. sequential
    C. locator   D. index

19. The MAIN purpose of a tickler file is to 19._____
    A. help prevent overlooking matters that require future attention
    B. check on adequacy of past performance
    C. pinpoint responsibility for recurring daily tasks
    D. reduce the volume of material kept in general files

20. Which of the following BEST describes the process of *reconciling* a bank statement? 20._____
    A. Analyzing the nature of the expenditures made by the office during the preceding month
    B. Comparing the statement of the bank with the banking records maintained in the office
    C. Determining the liquidity position by reading the bank statement carefully
    D. Checking the service charges noted on the bank statement

21. From the viewpoint of preserving agency or institutional funds, the LEAST acceptable method for making a payment is a check made out to 21._____
    A. cash   B. a company
    C. an individual   D. a partnership

22. Listed below are four of the steps in the process of preparing correspondence for filing. 22._____
    If they were to be put in logical sequence, the SECOND step would be
    A. preparing cross-reference sheets or cards
    B. coding the correspondence using a classification system
    C. sorting the correspondence in the order to be filed
    D. checking for follow-up action required and preparing a follow-up slip

23. The process of *justifying* typed copy involves laying out the copy so that
    A. each paragraph appears to be approximately the same size
    B. no long words are broken up at the end of a line
    C. the right and left hand margins are even
    D. there is enough room to enter proofreading marks at the end of each line

23._____

24. The MOST important reason for a person in charge of a petty cash fund to obtain receipts for payments is that this practice would tend to
    A. decrease robberies by delivery personnel
    B. eliminate the need to keep a record of petty cash expenditures
    C. prove that the fund has been used properly
    D. provide a record of the need for cash in the daily operations of the office

24._____

25. You should GENERALLY replenish a petty cash fund
    A. at regularly established intervals
    B. each time you withdraw a sum
    C. when the amount of cash gets below a certain specified amount
    D. when the fund is completely empty

25._____

KEY (CORRECT ANSWERS)

1. A	11. D	21. A
2. D	12. A	22. A
3. A	13. A	23. C
4. C	14. A	24. C
5. B	15. C	25. C
6. D	16. B	
7. C	17. C	
8. C	18. A	
9. D	19. A	
10. A	20. B	

EXAMINATION SECTION
TEST 1

DIRECTIONS: Each question or incomplete statement is followed by several suggested answers or completions. Select the one that BEST answers the question or completes the statement. *PRINT THE LETTER OF THE CORRECT ANSWER IN THE SPACE AT THE RIGHT.*

1. If you open a personal letter by mistake, the one of the following actions which it would generally be BEST for you to take is to

    A. ignore your error, attach the envelope to the letter, and distribute in the usual manner
    B. personally give the addressee the letter without any explanation
    C. place the letter inside the envelope, indicate under your initials that it was opened in error, and give to the addressee
    D. reseal the envelope or place the contents in another envelope and pass on to addressee

1.____

2. If you receive a telephone call regarding a matter which your office does not handle, you should FIRST

    A. give the caller the telephone number of the proper office so that he can dial again
    B. offer to transfer the caller to the proper office
    C. suggest that the caller re-dial since he probably dialed incorrectly
    D. tell the caller he has reached the wrong office and then hang up

2.____

3. When you answer the telephone, the MOST important reason for identifying yourself and your organization is to

    A. give the caller time to collect his or her thoughts
    B. impress the caller with your courtesy
    C. inform the caller that he or she has reached the right number
    D. set a business-like tone at the beginning of the conversation

3.____

4. The one of the following cases in which you would NOT place a special notation in the left margin of a letter that you have typed is when

    A. one of the copies is intended for someone other than the addressee of the letter
    B. you enclose a flyer with the letter
    C. you sign your superior's name to the letter, at his or her request
    D. the letter refers to something being sent under separate cover

4.____

5. Suppose that you accidentally cut a letter or enclosure as you are opening an envelope with a paper knife.
The one of the following that you should do FIRST is to

    A. determine whether the document is important
    B. clip or staple the pieces together and process as usual
    C. mend the cut document with transparent tape
    D. notify the sender that the communication was damaged and request another copy

5.____

13

6. As soon as you pick up the phone, a very angry caller begins immediately to complain about city agencies and *red tape*. He says that he has been shifted to two or three different offices. It turns out that he is seeking information which is not immediately available to you. You believe you know, however, where it can be found.
Which of the following actions is the BEST one for you to take?

   A. To eliminate all confusion, suggest that the caller write the mayor stating explicitly what he wants.
   B. Apologize by telling the caller how busy city agencies now are, but also tell him directly that you do not have the information he needs.
   C. Ask for the caller's telephone number, and assure him you will call back after you have checked further.
   D. Give the caller the name and telephone number of the person who might be able to help, but explain that you are not positive he will get results.

7. Suppose that one of your duties is to dictate responses to routine requests from the public for information. A letter writer asks for information which, as expressed in a one-sentence, explicit agency rule, cannot be given out to the public.
Of the following ways of answering the letter, which is the MOST efficient?

   A. Quote verbatim that section of the agency rules which prohibits giving this information to the public.
   B. Without quoting the rule, explain why you cannot accede to the request and suggest alternative sources.
   C. Describe how carefully the request was considered before classifying it as subject to the rule forbidding the issuance of such information.
   D. Acknowledge receipt of the letter and advise that the requested information is not released to the public.

8. Suppose you assist in supervising a staff which has rather high morale, and your own supervisor asks you to poll the staff to find out who will be able to work overtime this particular evening to help complete emergency work.
Which of the following approaches would be MOST likely to win their cooperation while maintaining their morale?

   A. Tell them that the better assignments will be given only to those who work overtime.
   B. Tell them that occasional overtime is a job requirement.
   C. Assure them they'll be doing you a personal favor.
   D. Let them know clearly why the overtime is needed.

9. Suppose that you have been asked to write and to prepare for reproduction new departmental vacation leave regulations.
After you have written the new regulations, all of which fit on two pages, which one of the following would be the BEST method of reproducing 1,000 copies?

   A. An outside private printer because you can best maintain confidentiality using this technique
   B. Photocopying because the copies will have the best possible appearance
   C. Sending the file to all department employees as printable PDFs
   D. Printing and collating on the office high-volume printer

10. You are in charge of verifying employees' qualifications. This involves telephoning previous employers and schools. One of the applications which you are reviewing contains information which you are almost certain is correct on the basis of what the employee has told you.
    The BEST thing to do is to

    A. check the information again with the employer
    B. perform the required verification procedures
    C. accept the information as valid
    D. ask a superior to verify the information

11. The practice of immediately identifying oneself and one's place of employment when contacting persons on the telephone is

    A. *good* because the receiver of the call can quickly identify the caller and establish a frame of reference
    B. *good* because it helps to set the caller at ease with the other party
    C. *poor* because it is not necessary to divulge that information when making general calls
    D. *poor* because it takes longer to arrive at the topic to be discussed

12. Which one of the following should be the MOST important overall consideration when preparing a recommendation to automate a large-scale office activity?
    The

    A. number of models of automated equipment available
    B. benefits and costs of automation
    C. fears and resistance of affected employees
    D. experience of offices which have automated similar activities

13. A tickler file is MOST appropriate for filing materials

    A. chronologically according to date they were received
    B. alphabetically by name
    C. alphabetically by subject
    D. chronologically according to date they should be followed up

14. Which of the following is the BEST reason for decentralizing rather then centralizing the use of duplicating machines?

    A. Developing and retaining efficient duplicating machine operators
    B. Facilitating supervision of duplicating services
    C. Motivating employees to produce legible duplicated copies
    D. Placing the duplicating machines where they are most convenient and most frequently used

15. Window envelopes are sometimes considered preferable to individually addressed envelopes PRIMARILY because

    A. window envelopes are available in standard sizes for all purposes
    B. window envelopes are more attractive and official-looking
    C. the use of window envelopes eliminates the risk of inserting a letter in the wrong envelope
    D. the use of window envelopes requires neater typing

16. In planning the layout of a new office, the utilization of space and the arrangement of staff, furnishings, and equipment should usually be MOST influenced by the

    A. gross square footage
    B. status differences in the chain of command
    C. framework of informal relationships among employees
    D. activities to be performed

17. Office forms sometimes consist of several copies, each of a different color. The MAIN reason for using different colors is to

    A. make a favorable impression on the users of the form
    B. distinguish each copy from the others
    C. facilitate the preparation of legible carbon copies
    D. reduce cost, since using colored stock permits recycling of paper

18. Which of the following is the BEST justification for obtaining a photocopying machine for the office?

    A. A photocopying machine can produce an unlimited number of copies at a low fixed cost per copy.
    B. Employees need little training in operating a photocopying machine.
    C. Office costs will be reduced and efficiency increased.
    D. The legibility of a photocopy generally is superior to copy produced by any other office duplicating device.

19. An administrative officer in charge of a small fund for buying office supplies has just written a check to Charles Laird, a supplier, and has sent the check by messenger to him. A half-hour later, the messenger telephones the administrative officer. He has lost the check.
Which of the following is the MOST important action for the administrative officer to take under these circumstances?

    A. Ask the messenger to return and write a report describing the loss of the check.
    B. Make a note on the performance record of the messenger who lost the check.
    C. Take the necessary steps to have payment stopped on the check.
    D. Refrain from doing anything since the check may be found shortly.

20. A petty cash fund is set up PRIMARILY to

    A. take care of small investments that must be made from time to time
    B. take care of small expenses that arise from time to time
    C. provide a fund to be used as the office wants to use it with little need to maintain records
    D. take care of expenses that develop during emergencies such as machine breakdowns and fires

21. Your superior has asked you to send a package from your agency to a government agency in another city. He has written out the message and has indicated the name of the government agency.
When you prepare the package for mailing, which of the following items that your superior has not mentioned must you be sure to include?

A. Today's date
B. The full address of the government agency
C. A polite opening such as *Dear Sirs*
D. A final sentence such as *We would appreciate hearing from your agency in reply as soon as is convenient for you*

22. In addition to the original piece of correspondence, one should USUALLY also have typed

    A. a single copy
    B. as many copies as can be typed at one time
    C. no more copies than are needed
    D. two copies

22.____

23. The one of the following which is the BEST procedure to follow when making a short insert in a completed dictation is to

    A. label the insert with a letter and indicate the position of the insert in the text by writing the identifying letter in the proper place
    B. squeeze the insert into its proper place within the main text of the dictation
    C. take down the insert and check the placement with the person who dictated when you are ready to transcribe your notes
    D. transcribe the dictation into longhand, including the insert in its proper position

23.____

24. The one of the following procedures which will be MOST efficient in helping you to quickly open your dictation notebook to a clean sheet is to

    A. clip or place a rubberband around the used portion of the notebook
    B. leave the book out and open to a clean page when not in use
    C. transcribe each dictation after it is given and rip out the used pages
    D. use a book marker to indicate which portion of the notebook has been used

24.____

25. The purpose of dating your dictation notebooks is GENERALLY to

    A. enable you to easily refer to your notes at a later date
    B. ensure that you transcribe your notes in the order in which they were dictated
    C. set up a precise record-keeping procedure
    D. show your employer that you pay attention to detail

25.____

KEY (CORRECT ANSWERS)

1.	C	11.	A
2.	B	12.	B
3.	C	13.	D
4.	C	14.	D
5.	C	15.	C
6.	C	16.	D
7.	A	17.	B
8.	D	18.	C
9.	D	19.	C
10.	B	20.	B

21. B
22. C
23. A
24. A
25. A

TEST 2

DIRECTIONS: Each question or incomplete statement is followed by several suggested answers or completions. Select the one that BEST answers the question or completes the statement. *PRINT THE LETTER OF THE CORRECT ANSWER IN THE SPACE AT THE RIGHT.*

1. With regard to typed correspondence received by most offices, which of the following is the GREATEST problem?

    A. Verbosity
    B. Illegibility
    C. Improper folding
    D. Excessive copies

    1.____

2. Of the following, the GREATEST advantage of flash drives over rewritable CD storage is that they

    A. are portable
    B. are both smaller and lighter
    C. contain more storage space
    D. allow files to be deleted to free space

    2.____

3. Suppose that a large quantity of information is in the files which are located a good distance from your desk. Almost every worker in your office must use these files constantly. Your duties in particular require that you daily refer to about 25 of the same items. They are short, one-page items distributed throughout the files. In this situation, your BEST course would be to

    A. take the items that you use daily from the files and keep them on your desk, inserting *out cards* in their place
    B. go to the files each time you need the information so that the items will be there when other workers need them
    C. make xerox copies of the information you use most frequently and keep them in your desk for ready reference
    D. label the items you use most often with different colored tabs for immediate identification

    3.____

4. Of the following, the MOST important advantage of preparing manuals of office procedures in loose-leaf form is that this form

    A. permits several employees to use different sections simultaneously
    B. facilitates the addition of new material and the removal of obsolete material
    C. is more readily arranged in alphabetical order
    D. reduces the need for cross-references to locate material carried under several headings

    4.____

5. Suppose that you establish a new clerical procedure for the unit you supervise. Your keeping a close check on the time required by your staff to handle the new procedure is WISE mainly because such a check will find out

    A. whether your subordinates know how to handle the new procedure
    B. whether a revision of the unit's work schedule will be necessary as a result of the new procedure
    C. what attitude your employees have toward the new procedure
    D. what alterations in job descriptions will be necessitated by the new procedure

    5.____

6. The numbered statements below relate to the stenographic skill of taking dictation. According to authorities on secretarial practices, which of these are generally recommended guides to development of efficient stenographic skills?

STATEMENTS
1. A stenographer should date her notebook daily to facilitate locating certain notes at a later time.
2. A stenographer should make corrections of grammatical mistakes while her boss is dictating to her.
3. A stenographer should draw a line through the dictated matter in her notebook after she has transcribed it.
4. A stenographer should write in longhand unfamiliar names and addresses dictated to her.

The CORRECT answer is:

A. Only Statements 1, 2, and 3 are generally recommended guides.
B. Only Statements 2, 3, and 4 are generally recommended guides.
C. Only Statements 1, 3, and 4 are generally recommended guides.
D. All four statements are generally recommended guides.

7. According to generally recognized rules of filing in an alphabetic filing system, the one of the following names which normally should be filed LAST is

A. Department of Education, New York State
B. F.B.I.
C. Police Department of New York City
D. P.S. 81 of New York City

8. Which one of the following forms for the typed name of the dictator in the closing lines of a letter is generally MOST acceptable in the United States?

A. (Dr.) James F. Fenton
B. Dr. James F. Fenton
C. Mr. James F. Fenton, Ph.D.
D. James F. Fenton

9. Which of the following is, MOST generally, a rule to be followed when typing a rough draft?

A. The copy should be single spaced.
B. The copy should be triple spaced.
C. There is no need for including footnotes.
D. Errors must be neatly corrected.

10. An office assistant needs a synonym.
Of the following, the book which she would find MOST useful is

A. a world atlas
B. BARTLETT'S FAMILIAR QUOTATIONS
C. a manual of style
D. a thesaurus

11. Of the following examples of footnotes, the one that is expressed in the MOST generally accepted standard form is:

    A. Johnson, T.F. (Dr.), English for Everyone, 3rd or 4th edition; New York City Linton Publishing Company, p. 467
    B. Frank Taylor, English for Today (New York: Rayton Publishing Company, 1971), p. 156
    C. Ralph Wilden, English for Tomorrow, Reynolds Publishing Company, England, p. 451
    D. Quinn, David, Yesterday's English (New York: Baldwin Publishing Company, 1972), p. 431

12. Standard procedures are used in offices PRIMARILY because

    A. an office is a happier place if everyone is doing the tasks in the same manner
    B. particular ways of doing jobs are considered more efficient than other ways
    C. it is good discipline for workers to follow standard procedures approved by the supervisor
    D. supervisors generally don't want workers to be creative in planning their work

13. Assume that an office assistant has the responsibility for compiling, typing, and mailing a preliminary announcement of Spring term course offerings. The announcement will go to approximately 900 currently enrolled students. Assuming that the following equipment is available for use, the MOST EFFECTIVE method for distributing the announcement to all 900 students is to

    A. e-mail it as a text document using the electronic student mailing list
    B. post the announcement as a PDF document for download on the department website
    C. send it by fax
    D. post the announcement and leave copies in buildings around campus

14. *Justified typing* is a term that refers MOST specifically to typewriting copy

    A. that has been edited and for which final copy is being prepared
    B. in a form that allows for an even right-hand margin
    C. with a predetermined vertical placement for each alternate line
    D. that has been approved by the supervisor and his superior

15. Which one of the following is the BEST form for the address in a letter?

    A. Mr. John Jones
       Vice President, The Universal Printing Company
       1220 Fifth Avenue
       New York, 10023 New York
    B. Mr. John Jones, Vice President
       The Universal Printing Company
       1220 Fifth Avenue
       New York, New York 10023
    C. Mr. John Jones, Vice President, The Universal Printing Company
       1220 Fifth Avenue
       New York, New York 10023

D. Mr. John Jones Vice President,
The Universal Printing Company
1220 Fifth Avenue
New York, 10023 New York

16. Of the following, the CHIEF advantage of the use of window envelopes over ordinary envelopes is that window envelopes

    A. eliminate the need for addressing envelopes
    B. protect the confidential nature of enclosed material
    C. cost less to buy than ordinary envelopes
    D. reduce the danger of the address becoming illegible

17. In the complimentary close of a business letter, the FIRST letter of _____ should be capitalized.

    A. all the words
    B. none of the words
    C. only the first word
    D. only the last word

18. Assume that one of your duties is to procure needed office supplies from the supply room. You are permitted to draw supplies every two weeks.
    The one of the following which would be the MOST desirable practice for you to follow in obtaining supplies is to

    A. obtain a quantity of supplies sufficient to last for several months to make certain that enough supplies are always on hand
    B. determine the minimum supply necessary to keep on hand for the various items and obtain an additional quantity as soon as possible after the supply on hand has been reduced to this minimum
    C. review the supplies once a month to determine what items have been exhausted and obtain an additional quantity as soon as possible
    D. obtain a supply of an item as soon after it has been exhausted as is possible

19. Some offices that keep carbon copies of letters use several different colors of carbon paper for making carbon copies.
    Of the following, the CHIEF reason for using different colors of carbon paper is to

    A. facilitate identification of different types of letters in the files
    B. relieve the monotony of typing and filing carbon copies
    C. reduce the costs of preparing carbon copies
    D. utilize both sides of the carbon paper for typing

20. Your supervisor asks you to post an online ad for freelance designers interested in submitting samples for a new company logo. Prospective workers should be proficient in which of the following software?

    A. Microsoft Word
    B. Adobe Acrobat Pro
    C. Adobe Illustrator
    D. Microsoft PowerPoint

21. Gary Thompson is applying for a position with the firm of Gray and Williams.
    Which letter should be filed in top position in the *Application* folder?

    A. A letter of recommendation written on September 18 by Johnson & Smith
    B. Williams' letter of October 8 requesting further details regarding Thompson's experience

C. Thompson's letter of September 8 making application for a position as sales manager
D. Letter of September 20 from Alfred Jackson recommending Thompson for the job

22. The USUAL arrangement in indexing the names of the First National Bank, Toledo, is

    A. First National Bank, Toledo, Ohio
    B. Ohio, First National Bank, Toledo
    C. Toledo, First National Bank, Ohio
    D. Ohio, Toledo, First National Bank

23. A single line through typed text indicating that it's incorrect or invalid is known as a(n)

    A. underline
    B. strikethrough
    C. line font
    D. eraser

24. A typical e-mail with an attachment should contain all of the following for successful transmittal EXCEPT

    A. recipient's address
    B. file attachment
    C. body text
    D. description of attachment

25. The subject line in a letter is USUALLY typed a _____ space below the _____.

    A. single; inside address
    B. single; salutation
    C. double; inside address
    D. double; salutation

KEY (CORRECT ANSWERS)

1. A		11. B	
2. C		12. B	
3. C		13. A	
4. B		14. B	
5. B		15. B	
6. C		16. A	
7. D		17. C	
8. D		18. B	
9. B		19. A	
10. D		20. C	

21. B
22. A
23. B
24. D
25. D

EXAMINATION SECTION
TEST 1

DIRECTIONS: Each question or incomplete statement is followed by several suggested answers or completions. Select the one that BEST answers the question or completes the statement. *PRINT THE LETTER OF THE CORRECT ANSWER IN THE SPACE AT THE RIGHT.*

1. Assume that a few co-workers meet near your desk and talk about personal matters during working hours. Lately, this practice has interfered with your work. In order to stop this practice, the BEST action for you to take FIRST is to
    A. ask your supervisor to put a stop to the co-workers' meeting near your desk
    B. discontinue any friendship with this group
    C. ask your co-workers not to meet near your desk
    D. request that your desk be moved to another location

1.____

2. In order to maintain office coverage during working hours, your supervisor has scheduled your lunch hour from 1 P.M. to 2 P.M. and your co-workers' lunch hour from 12 P.M. to 1 P.M. Lately, your co-worker has been returning late from lunch each day. As a result, you don't get a full hour since you must return to the office by 2 P.M.
Of the following, the BEST action for you to take FIRST is to
    A. explain to your co-worker in a courteous manner that his lateness is interfering with your right to a full hour for lunch
    B. tell your co-worker that his lateness must stop or you will report him to your supervisor
    C. report your co-worker's lateness to your supervisor
    D. leave at 1 P.M. for lunch, whether your co-worker has returned or not

2.____

3. Assume that, as an office worker, one of your jobs is to open mail sent to your unit, read the mail for content, and send the mail to the appropriate person to handle. You accidentally open and begin to read a letter marked *personal* to a co-worker.
Of the following, the BEST action for you to take is to
    A. report to your supervisor that your co-worker is receiving personal mail at the office
    B. destroy the letter so that your co-worker does not know you saw it
    C. reseal the letter and place it on the co-worker's desk without saying anything
    D. bring the letter to your co-worker and explain that you opened it by accident

3.____

4. Suppose that in evaluating your work, your supervisor gives you an overall rating, but states that you sometimes turn in work with careless errors. 4.____
   The BEST action for you to take would be to
   A. ask a co-worker who is good at details to proofread your work
   B. take time to do a careful job, paying more attention to detail
   C. continue working as usual since occasional errors are to be expected
   D. ask your supervisor if she would mind correcting your errors

5. Assume that you are taking a telephone message for a co-worker who is not in the office at the time. 5.____
   Of the following, the LEAST important item to write on the message is the
   A. length of the call   B. name of the caller
   C. time of the call   D. telephone number of the caller

Questions 6-13.

DIRECTIONS: Questions 6 through 13 each consist of a sentence which may or may not be an example of good English. The underlined parts of each sentence may be correct or incorrect. Examine each sentence, considering grammar, punctuation, spelling, and capitalization. If the English usage in the underlined parts of the sentence given is better than any of the changes in the underlined words suggested in Options B, C, or D, choose Option A. If the changes in the underlined words suggested in Options B, C, or D would make the sentence correct, choose the correct option. Do not choose an option that will change the meaning of the sentence.

6. This Fall, the office will be closed on Columbus Day, October 9th. 6.____
   A. Correct as is   B. fall...Columbus Day, October
   C. Fall...Columbus day, October D. fall...Columbus Day, october

7. This manual discribes the duties performed by an Office Aide. 7.____
   A. Correct as is   B. describe the duties performed
   C. discribe the duties performed D. describes the duties performed

8. There weren't no paper in the supply closet. 8.____
   A. Correct as is   B. weren't any
   C. wasn't any   D. wasn't no

9. The new employees left there office to attend a meeting. 9.____
   A. Correct as is   B. they're
   C. their   D. thier

10. The office worker started working at 8:30 a.m. 10.____
    A. Correct as is   B. 8:30 a.m.
    C. 8;30 a,m.   D. 8:30 am.

11. The alphabet, or A to Z sequence are the basis of most filing systems. 11.____
    A. Correct as is   B. alphabet, or A to Z sequence, is
    C. alphabet, or A to Z sequence are   D. alphabet, or A too Z sequence, is

12. Those file cabinets are five feet tall. 12.____
    A. Correct as is   B. Them…feet
    C. Those…foot   D. Them…foot

13. The Office Aide checked the register and finding the date of the meeting. 13.____
    A. Correct as is   B. regaster and finding
    C. register and found   D. regaster and found

Questions 14-21.

DIRECTIONS: Each of Questions 14 through 21 has two lists of numbers. Each list contains three sets of numbers. Check each of the three sets in the list on the right to see if they are the same as the corresponding set in the list on the left. Mark your answers
  A. if none of the sets in the right list are the same as those in the left list
  B. if only one of the sets in the right list are the same as those in the left list
  C. if only two of the sets in the right list are the same as those in the left list
  D. if all three sets in the right list are the same as those in the left list

14. 7354183476   7354983476   14.____
     4474747744   4474747774
     57914302311   57914302311

15. 7143592185   7143892185   15.____
     8344517699   8344518699
     9178531263   9178531263

16. 2572114731   257214731   16.____
     8806835476   8806835476
     8255831246   8255831246

17. 331476853821   331476858621   17.____
     6976658532996   6976655832996
     3766042113715   3766042113745

18. 8806663315   8806663315   18.____
     74477138449   74477138449
     211756663666   211756663666

19. 990006966996   99000696996   19.____
     53022219743   53022219843
     4171171117717   4171171177717

20. 24400222433004   24400222433004   20.____
     5300030055000355 5300030055500355
     20000075532002022 20000075532002022

4 (#1)

21. 6111666406600011166   61116664066001116   21._____
     7111300117001100733   7111300117001100733
     26666446664476518   26666446664476518

Questions 22-25.

DIRECTIONS: Each of Questions 22 through 25 has two lists of names and addresses. Each
list contains three sets of names and addresses. Check each of the three sets
in the list on the right to see if they are the same as the corresponding set in
the list on the left. Mark your answers
  A. if none of the sets in the right list are the same as those in the left list
  B. if only one of the sets in the right list are the same as those in the left list
  C. if only two of the sets in the right list are the same as those in the left list
  D. if all three sets in the right list are the same as those in the left list

22. Mary T. Berlinger   Mary T. Berlinger   22._____
     2351 Hampton St.   2351 Hampton St.
     Monsey, N.Y. 20117   Monsey, N.Y. 20117

     Eduardo Benes   Eduardo Benes
     473 Kingston Avenue   473 Kingston Avenue
     Central Islip, N.Y. 11734   Central Islip, N.Y. 11734

     Alan Carrington Fuchs   Alan Carrington Fuchs
     17 Gnarled Hollow Road   17 Gnarled Hollow Road
     Los Angeles, CA 91635   Los Angeles, CA 91685

23. David John Jacobson   David John Jacobson   23._____
     178 35 St. Apt. 4C   178 53 St. Apt. 4C
     New York, N.Y. 00927   New York, N.Y. 00927

     Ann-Marie Calonella   Ann-Marie Calonella
     7243 South Ridge Blvd.   7243 South Ridge Blvd.
     Bakersfield, CA 96714   Bakersfield, CA 96714

     Pauline M. Thompson   Pauline M. Thomson
     872 Linden Ave.   872 Linden Ave.
     Houston, Texas 70321   Houston, Texas 70321

24. Chester LeRoy Masterton   Chester LeRoy Masterson   24._____
     152 Lacy Rd.   152 Lacy Rd.
     Kankakee, Ill. 54532   Kankakee, Ill. 54532

     William Maloney   William Maloney
     S. LaCrosse Pla.   S. LaCross Pla.
     Wausau, Wisconsin 52146   Wausau, Wisconsin 52146

5 (#1)

	Cynthia V. Barnes 16 Pines Rd. Greenpoint, Miss. 20376	Cynthia V. Barnes 16 Pines Rd. Greenpoint, Miss. 20376	
25.	Marcel Jean Frontenac 6 Burton On The Water Calender, Me. 01471	Marcel Jean Frontenac 6 Burton On The Water Calender, Me. 01471	25.____
	J. Scott Marsden 174 S. Tipton St. Cleveland, Ohio	J. Scott Marsden 174 Tipton St. Cleveland, Ohio	
	Lawrence T. Haney 171 McDonough St. Decatur, Ga. 31304	Lawrence T. Haney 171 McDonough St. Decatur, Ga. 31304	

KEY (CORRECT ANSWERS)

1.	C		11.	B
2.	A		12.	A
3.	D		13.	C
4.	B		14.	B
5.	A		15.	B
6.	B		16.	C
7.	D		17.	A
8.	C		18.	D
9.	C		19.	A
10.	B		20.	C

21. C
22. C
23. B
24. B
25. C

TEST 2

DIRECTIONS: Each question or incomplete statement is followed by several suggested answers or completions. Select the one that BEST answers the question or completes the statement. *PRINT THE LETTER OF THE CORRECT ANSWER IN THE SPACE AT THE RIGHT.*

Questions 1-6.

DIRECTIONS: Questions 1 through 6 are to be answered SOLELY on the basis of the information contained in the following passage.

Duplicating is the process of making a number of identical copies of letters, document, etc. from an original. Some duplicating processes make copies directly from the original document. Other duplicating processes require the preparation of a special master, and copies are then made from the master. Four of the most common duplicating processes are stencil, fluid, offset, and xerox.

In the stencil process, the typewriter is used to cut the words into a master called a stencil. Drawings, charts, or graphs can be cut into the stencil using a stylus. As many as 3,500 good-quality copies can be reproduced from one stencil. Various grades of finished paper from inexpensive mimeograph to expensive bond can be used.

The fluid process is a good method of copying from 50 to 125 good-quality copies from a master, which is prepared with a special dye. The master is placed on the duplicator, and special paper with a hard finish is moistened and then passed through the duplicator. Some of the dye on the master is dissolved, creating an impression on the paper. The impression becomes lighter as more copies are made; and once the dye on the master is used up, a new master must be made.

The offset process is the most adaptable office duplicating process because this process can be used for making a few copies or many copies. Masters can be made on paper or plastic for a few hundred copies, or on metal plates for as many as 75,000 copies. By using a special technique called photo-offset, charts, photographs, illustrations, or graphs can be reproduced on the master plate. The offset process is capable of producing large quantities of fine, top-quality copies on all types of finished paper.

The xerox process reproduces an exact duplicate from an original. It is the fastest duplicating method because the original material is placed directly on the duplicator, eliminating the need to make a special master. Any kind of paper can be used. The xerox process is the most expensive duplicating process; however, it is the best method of reproducing small quantities of good-quality copies of reports, letters, official documents, memos, or contracts.

1. Of the following, the MOST efficient method of reproducing 5,000 copies of a graph is
   A. stencil   B. fluid   C. offset   D. xerox

1.____

2. The offset process is the MOST adaptable office duplicating process because
   A. it is the quickest duplicating method
   B. it is the least expensive duplicating method
   C. it can produce a small number or large number of copies
   D. a softer master can be used over and over again

3. Which one of the following duplicating processes uses moistened paper?
   A. Stencil   B. Fluid   C. Offset   D. Xerox

4. The fluid process would be the BEST process to use for reproducing
   A. five copies of a school transcript
   B. fifty copies of a memo
   C. five hundred copies of a form letter
   D. five thousand copies of a chart

5. Which one of the following duplicating processes does NOT require a special master?
   A. Fluid   B. Xerox   C. Offset   D. Stencil

6. Xerox is NOT used for all duplicating jobs because
   A. it produces poor-quality copies
   B. the process is too expensive
   C. preparing the master is too time-consuming
   D. it cannot produce written reports

7. Assume a city agency has 775 office workers.
   If 2 out of 25 office workers were absent on a particular day, how many office workers reported to work on that day?
   A. 713   B. 744   C. 750   D. 773

Questions 8-11,

DIRECTIONS: In Questions 8 through 11, select the choice that is CLOSEST in meaning to the underlined word.

   SAMPLE: This division reviews the fiscal reports of the agency.
              In this sentence, the word *fiscal* means MOST NEARLY
              A. financial   B. critical   C. basic   D. personnel

   The correct answer is A, financial, because financial is closest to *fiscal*.

8. A central file eliminates the need to retain duplicate material.
   The word *retain* means MOST NEARLY
   A. keep   B. change   C. locate   D. process

9. Filing is a routine office task.
   Routine means MOST NEARLY
   A. proper   B. regular   C. simple   D. difficult

10. Sometimes a word, phrase, or sentence must be <u>deleted</u> to correct an error. 10.____
    Deleted means MOST NEARLY
    A. removed   B. added   C. expanded   D. improved

11. Your supervisor will <u>evaluate</u> your work. 11.____
    Evaluate means MOST NEARLY
    A. judge   B. list   C. assign   D. explain

Questions 12-19.

DIRECTIONS: The code table below shows 10 letters with matching numbers. For each Question 12 through 19, there are three sets of letters. Each set of letters is followed by a set of numbers which may or may not match their correct letter according to the code table. For each question, check all three sets of letters and numbers and mark your answer
 A. if no pairs are correctly matched
 B. if only one pair is correctly matched
 C. if only two pairs are correctly matched
 D. if all three pairs are correctly matched

<u>CODE TABLE</u>

T	M	V	D	S	P	R	G	B	H
1	2	3	4	5	6	7	8	9	0

SAMPLE QUESTION: TMVDSP 123456
                  RGBHTM 789011
                  DSPRGB 256789

In the sample question above, the first set of numbers correctly matches its set of letters. But the second and third pairs contain mistakes. In the second pair, M is incorrectly matched with number 1. According to the code table, letter M should be correctly matched with number 2. In the third pair, the letter D is incorrectly matched with number 2. According to the code table, letter D should be correctly matched with number 4. Since only one of the pairs is correctly matched, the answer to this sample question is B.

12. RSBMRM   759262   12.____
    GDSRVH   845730
    VDBRTM   349713

13. TGVSDR   183247   13.____
    SMHRDP   520647
    TRMHSR   172057

14. DSPRGM   456782   14.____
    MVDBHT   234902
    HPMDBT   062491

15.	BVPTRD	936184	15._____
	GDPHMB	807029	
	GMRHMV	827032	
16.	MGVRSH	283750	16._____
	TRDMBS	174295	
	SPRMGV	567283	
17.	SGBSDM	489542	17._____
	MGHPTM	290612	
	MPBMHT	269301	
18.	TDPBHM	146902	18._____
	VPBMRS	369275	
	GDMBHM	842902	
19.	MVPTBV	236194	19._____
	PDRTMB	647128	
	BGTMSM	981232	

Questions 20-25.

DIRECTIONS: In each of Questions 20 through 25, the names of four people are given. For each question, choose as your answer the one of the four names given which should be filed FIRST according to the usual system of alphabetical filing of names, as described in the following paragraph.

In filing names, you must start with the last name. Names are filed in order of the first letter of the last name, then the second letter, etc. Therefore, BAILY would be filed before BROWN, which would be filed before COLT. A name with fewer letters of the same type comes first; i.e., Smith before Smithe. If the last names are the same, the names are filed alphabetically by the first name. If the first name is an initial, a name with an initial would come before a first name that starts with the same letter as the initial. Therefore, I. BROWN would come before IRA BROWN. Finally, if both last name and first name are the same, the name would be filed alphabetically by the middle name, one again an initial coming before a middle name which starts with the same letter as the initial. If there is no middle name at all, the name would come before those with middle initials or names.

SAMPLE QUESTION: A. Lester Daniels
B. William Dancer
C. Nathan Danzig
D. Dan Lester

The last names beginning with D are filed before the last name beginning with L. Since DANIELS, DANCER, and DANZIG all begin with the same three letters, you must look at the fourth letter of the last name to determine which name should be filed first. C comes before I or Z in the alphabet, so DANCER is filed before DANIELS or DANZIG. Therefore, the answer to the above sample question is B.

5 (#2)

20. A. Scott Biala B. Mary Byala 20.____
    C. Martin Baylor D. Francis Bauer

21. A. Howard J. Black B. Howard Black 21.____
    C. J. Howard Black D. John H. Black

22. A. Theodora Garth Kingston B. Theadore Barth Kingston 22.____
    C. Thomas Kingston D. Thomas T. Kingston

23. A. Paulette Mary Huerta B. Paul M. Huerta 23.____
    C. Paulette L. Huerta D. Peter A. Huerta

24. A. Martha Hunt Morgan B. Martin Hunt Morgan 24.____
    C. Mary H. Morgan D. Martine H. Morgan

25. A. James T. Meerschaum B. James M. Mershum 25.____
    C. James F. Mearshaum D. James N. Meshum

KEY (CORRECT ANSWERS)

1.	C	11.	A
2.	C	12.	B
3.	B	13.	B
4.	B	14.	C
5.	B	15.	A
6.	B	16.	D
7.	A	17.	A
8.	A	18.	D
9.	B	19.	A
10.	A	20.	D

21. B
22. B
23. B
24. A
25. C

TEST 3

DIRECTIONS: Each question or incomplete statement is followed by several suggested answers or completions. Select the one that BEST answers the question or completes the statement. *PRINT THE LETTER OF THE CORRECT ANSWER IN THE SPACE AT THE RIGHT.*

1. Which one of the following statements about proper telephone usage is NOT always correct?
   When answering the telephone, you should
   A. know whom you are speaking to
   B. give the caller your undivided attention
   C. identify yourself to the caller
   D. obtain the information the caller wishes before you do your other work

   1.____

2. Assume that, as a member of a worker's safety committee in your agency, you are responsible for encouraging other employees to follow correct safety practices. While you are working on your regular assignment, you observe an employee violating a safety rule.
   Of the following, the BEST action for you to take FIRST is to
   A. speak to the employee about safety practices and order him to stop violating the safety rule
   B. speak to the employee about safety practices and point out the safety rule he is violating
   C. bring the matter up in the next committee meeting
   D. report this violation of the safety rule to the employee's supervisor

   2.____

3. Assume that you have been temporarily assigned by your supervisor to do a job which you do not want to do.
   The BEST action for you to take is to
   A. discuss the job with your supervisor, explaining why you do not want to do it
   B. discuss the job with your supervisor and tell her that you will not do it
   C. ask a co-worker to take your place on this job
   D. do some other job that you like; your supervisor may give the job you do not like to someone else

   3.____

4. Assume that you keep the confidential personnel files of employees in your unit. A friend asks you to obtain some information from the file of one of your co-workers.
   The BEST action to take is to _____ to your friend.
   A. ask the co-worker if you can give the information
   B. ask your supervisor if you can give the information
   C. give the information
   D. refuse to give the information

   4.____

35

Questions 5-8.

DIRECTIONS: Questions 5 through 8 are to be answered SOLELY on the basis of the information contained in the following passage.

City government is committed to providing a safe and healthy work environment for all city employees. An effective agency safety program reduces accidents by educating employees about the types of careless acts which can cause accidents. Even in an office, accidents can happen. If each employee is aware of possible safety hazards, the number of accidents on the job can be reduced.

Careless use of office equipment can cause accidents and injuries. For example, file cabinet drawers which are filled with papers can be so heavy that the entire cabinet could tip over from the weight of one open drawer.

The bottom drawers of desks and file cabinets should never be left open since employees can easily trip over open drawers and injure themselves.

When reaching for objects on a high shelf, an employee should use a strong, sturdy object such as a stepstool to stand on. Makeshift platforms made out of books, papers, or boxes can easily collapse. Even chairs can slide out from under foot, causing serious injury.

Even at an employee's desk, safety hazards can occur. Frayed or cut wires should be repaired or replaced immediately. Computers which are not firmly anchored to the desk or table could fall, causing injury.

Smoking is one of the major causes of fires in the office. A lighted match or improperly extinguished cigarette thrown into a wastebasket filled with paper could cause a major fire with possible loss of life. Where smoking is permitted, ashtrays should be used. Smoking is particularly dangerous in offices were flammable chemicals are used.

5. The goal of an effective safety program is to
    A. reduce office accidents
    B. stop employees from smoking on the job
    C. encourage employees to continue their education
    D. eliminate high shelves in offices

6. Desks and file cabinets can become safety hazards when
    A. their drawers are left open
    B. they are used as wastebaskets
    C. they are makeshift
    D. they are not anchored securely to the floor

7. Smoking is especially hazardous when it occurs
    A. near exposed wires
    B. in a crowded office
    C. in an area where flammable chemicals are used
    D. where books and papers are stored

8. Accidents are likely to occur when
    A. employees' desks are cluttered with books and papers
    B. employees are not aware of safety hazards
    C. employees close desk drawers
    D. stepstools are used to reach high objects

9. Assume that part of your job as a worker in the accounting division of a city agency is to answer the telephone.
   When you first answer the telephone, it is LEAST important to tell the caller
   A. your title
   B. your name
   C. the name of your unit
   D. the name of your agency

10. Assume that you are assigned to work as a receptionist, and your duties are to answer phones, greet visitors, and do other general office work. You are busy with a routine job when several visitors approach your desk.
    The BEST action to take is to
    A. ask the visitors to have a seat and assist them after your work is completed
    B. tell the visitors that you are busy and they should return at a more convenient time
    C. stop working long enough to assist the visitors
    D. continue working and wait for the visitors to ask you for assistance

11. Assume that your supervisor has chosen you to take a special course during hours to learn a new payroll procedure. Although you know that you were chosen because of your good work record, a co-worker, who feels that he should have been chosen, has been telling everyone in your unit that the choice was unfair.
    Of the following, the BEST way to handle this situation FIRST is to
    A. suggest to the co-worker that everything in life is unfair
    B. contact your union representative in case your co-worker presents a formal grievance
    C. tell your supervisor about your co-worker's complaints and let her handle the situation
    D. tell the co-worker that you were chosen because of your superior work record

12. Assume that while you are working on an assignment which must be completed quickly, a supervisor from another unit asks you to obtain information for her.
    Of the following, the BEST way to respond to her request is to
    A. tell her to return in an hour since you are busy
    B. give her the names of some people in her own unit who could help her
    C. tell her you are busy and refer her to a co-worker
    D. tell her that you are busy and ask her if she could wait until you finish your assignment

13. A co-worker in your unit is often off from work because of illness. Your supervisor assigns the co-worker's work to you when she is not there. Lately, doing her work has interfered with your own job.
    The BEST action for you to take FIRST is to
    A. discuss the problem with your supervisor
    B. complete your own work before starting your co-worker's work
    C. ask other workers in your unit to assist you
    D. work late in order to get the jobs done

14. During the month of June, 40,587 people attended a city-owned swimming pool. In July, 13,014 more people attended the swimming pool than the number that had attended in June. In August, 39,655 people attended the swimming pool. The TOTAL number of people who attended the swimming pool during the months of June, July, and August was

    A. 80,242   B. 93,256   C. 133,843   D. 210,382

14.____

Questions 15-22.

DIRECTIONS: Questions 15 through 22 test how well you understand what you read. It will be necessary for you to read carefully because your answers to these questions must be based ONLY on the information in the following paragraphs.

    The telephone directory is made up of two books. The first book consists of the introductory section and the alphabetical listing of names section. The second book is the classified directory (also known as the yellow pages). Many people who are familiar with one book do not realize how useful the other can be. The efficient office worker should become familiar with both books in order to make the best use of this important source of information.
    The introductory section gives general instructions for finding numbers in the alphabetical listing and classified directory. This section also explains how to use the telephone company's many services, including the operator and information services, gives examples of charges for local and long-distance calls, and lists area codes for the entire country. In addition, this section provides a useful zip code map.
    The alphabetical listing of names section lists the names, addresses, and telephone numbers of subscribers in an area. Guide names, or *telltales*, are on the top corner of each page. These guide names indicate the first and last name to be found on that page. *Telltales* help locate any particular name quickly. A cross-reference spelling is also given to help locate names which are spelled several different ways. City, state, and federal government agencies are listed under the major government heading. For example, an agency of the federal government would be listed under *United States Government*.
    The classified directory, or yellow pages, is a separate book. In this section are advertising services, public transportation line maps, shopping guides, and listings of businesses arranged by the type of product or services they offer. This book is most useful when looking for the name or phone number of a business when all that is known is the type of product offered and the address, or when trying to locate a particular type of business in an area. Businesses listed in the classified directory can usually be found in the alphabetical listing of names section. When the name of the business is known, you will find the address or phone number more quickly in the alphabetical listing of names section.

15. The introductory section provides

    A. shopping guides   B. government listings
    C. business listings   D. information services

15.____

16. Advertising services would be found in the

    A. introductory section   B. alphabetical listing of names section\
    C. classified directory   D. information services

16.____

17. According to the information in the above passage for locating government agencies, the Information Office of the Department of Consumer Affairs of New York City government would be alphabetically listed FIRST under
    A. *I* for Information Offices
    B. *D* for Department of Consumer Affairs
    C. *N* for New York City
    D. *G* for government

17.____

18. When the name of a business is known, the QUICKEST way to find the phone number is to look in the
    A. classified directory
    B. introductory section
    C. alphabetical listing of name section
    D. advertising service section

18.____

19. The QUICKEST way to find the phone number of a business when the type of service a business offers and its address is known is to look in the
    A. classified directory
    B. alphabetical listing of names section
    C. introductory section
    D. information service

19.____

20. What is a *telltale*?
    A. An alphabetical listing
    B. A guide name
    C. A map
    D. A cross-reference listing

20.____

21. The BEST way to find a postal zip code is to look in the
    A. classified directory
    B. introductory section
    C. alphabetical listing of names section
    D. government heading

21.____

22. To help find names which have several different spellings, the telephone directory provides
    A. cross-reference spelling
    B. *telltales*
    C. spelling guides
    D. advertising services

22.____

23. Assume that your agency has been given $2,025 to purchase file cabinets. If each file cabinet costs $135, how many file cabinet can your agency purchase?
    A. 8   B. 10   C. 15   D. 16

23.____

24. Assume that your unit ordered 14 staplers at a total cost of $30.20 and each stapler cost the same.
    The cost of one stapler was MOST NEARLY
    A. $1.02   B. $1.61   C. $2.16   D. $2.26

24.____

25. Assume that you are responsible for counting and recording licensing fees collected by your department. On a particular day, your department collected in fees 40 checks in the amount of $6 each, 80 checks in the amount of $4 each, 45 twenty dollar bills, 30 ten dollar bills, 42 five dollar bills, and 186 one dollar bills.
The TOTAL amount in fees collected on that day was
   A. $1,406   B. $1,706   C. $2,156   D. $2,356

26. Assume that you are responsible for your agency's petty cash fund. During the month of February, you pay out 7 $2.00 subway fares and one taxi fare for $10.85. You pay out nothing else from the fund. At the end of February, you count the money left in the fund and find 3 one dollar bills, 4 quarters, 5 dimes, and 4 nickels.
The amount of money you had available in the petty cash fund at the BEGINNING of February was
   A. $4.70   B. $16.35   C. $24.85   D. $29.55

27. You overhear your supervisor criticize a co-worker for handling equipment in an unsafe way. You feel that the criticism may be unfair.
Of the following, it would be BEST for you to
   A. take your co-worker aside and tell her how you feel about your supervisor's comments
   B. interrupt the discussion and defend your co-worker to your supervisor
   C. continue working as if you had not overheard the discussion
   D. make a list of other workers who have violated safety rules and give it to your supervisor

28. Assume that you have been assigned to work on a long-term project with an employee who is known for being uncooperative.
In beginning to work with this employee, it would be LEAST desirable for you to
   A. understand why the person is uncooperative
   B. act in a calm manner rather than an emotional manner
   C. be appreciative of the co-worker's work
   D. report the co-worker's lack of cooperation to your supervisor

29. Assume that you are assigned to sell tickets at a city-owned ice skating rink. An adult ticket costs $4.50, and a children's ticket costs $2.25. At the end of a day, you find that you have sold 36 adult tickets and 80 children's tickets.
The TOTAL amount of money you collected for that day was
   A. $244.80   B. $318.00   C. $342.00   D. $348.00

30. If each office worker files 487 index cards in one hour, how many card can 26 office workers file in one hour?
   A. 10,662   B. 12,175   C. 12,662   D. 14,266

KEY (CORRECT ANSWERS)

1.	D	11.	C	21.	B
2.	B	12.	D	22.	A
3.	A	13.	A	23.	C
4.	D	14.	C	24.	C
5.	A	15.	D	25.	C
6.	A	16.	C	26.	D
7.	C	17.	C	27.	C
8.	B	18.	C	28.	D
9.	A	19.	A	29.	C
10.	C	20.	B	30.	C

EXAMINATION SECTION
TEST 1

DIRECTIONS: Each question or incomplete statement is followed by several suggested answers or completions. Select the one that BEST answers the question or completes the statement. *PRINT THE LETTER OF THE CORRECT ANSWER IN THE SPACE AT THE RIGHT.*

1. A multi-line telephone with buttons for eight separate lines, plus a *hold* button, is often used when an office requires more than one outside line.
   If you are talking on one line of this type of office phone when another call comes in, what is the procedure to follow if you want to answer the second call but keep the first call on the line?
   Push the
   A. *hold* button at the same time as you push the *pickup* button of the ringing line
   B. *hold* button and then push the *pickup* button of the ringing line
   C. *pickup* button of the ringing line and then push the *hold* button
   D. *pickup* button of the ringing line and push the *hold* button when you return to the original line

   1._____

2. Suppose that you are asked to prepare a petty cash statement for March. The original and one copy are to go to the personnel office. One copy is to go to the fiscal office, and another copy is to go to your supervisor. The last copy is for your files.
   In preparing the statement and the copies, how many sheets of copy paper should you use?
   A. 3   B. 4   C. 5   D. 8

   2._____

3. Which one of the following is the LEAST important advantage of putting the subject of a letter in the heading to the right of the address? It
   A. makes filing of the copy easier
   B. makes more space available in the body of the letter
   C. simplifies distribution of letters
   D. simplifies determination of the subject of the letter

   3._____

4. Of the following, the MOST efficient way to put 100 copies of a one-page letter into 9½" x 4⅛" envelopes for mailing is to fold _____ into an envelope.
   A. each letter and insert it immediately after folding
   B. each letter separately until all 100 are folded; then insert each one
   C. the 100 letters two at a time, then separate them and insert each one
   D. two letters together, slip them apart, and insert each one

   4._____

5. When preparing papers for filing, it is NOT desirable to
   A. smooth papers that are wrinkled
   B. use paper clips to keep related papers together in the files
   C. arrange the papers in the order in which they will be filed
   D. mend torn papers with cellophane tape

6. Of the following, the BEST reason for a clerical unit to have its own duplicating machine is that the unit
   A. uses many forms which it must reproduce internally
   B. must make two copies of each piece of incoming mail for a special file
   C. must make seven copies of each piece of outgoing mail
   D. must type 200 envelopes each month for distribution to the same offices

7. Several offices use the same photocopying machine.
   If each office must pay its share of the cost of running this machine, the BEST way of determining how much of this cost should be charged to each of these offices is to
   A. determine the monthly number of photocopies made by each office
   B. determine the monthly number of originals submitted for photocopying by each office
   C. determine the number of times per day each office uses the photocopying machine
   D. divide the total cost of running the photocopy machine by the total number of offices using the machine

8. Which one of the following would it be BEST to use to indicate that a file folder has been removed from the files for temporary use in another office?
   A(n)
   A. cross-reference card   B. tickler file marker
   C. aperture card   D. out guide

9. Which one of the following is the MOST important objective of filing?
   A. Giving a secretary something to do in her spare time
   B. Making it possible to locate information quickly
   C. Providing a place to store unneeded documents
   D. Keeping extra papers from accumulating on workers' desks

10. If a check has been made out for an incorrect amount, the BEST action for the writer of the check to take is to
    A. erase the original amount and enter the correct amount
    B. cross out the original amount with a single line and enter the correct amount above it
    C. black out the original amount so that it cannot be read and enter the correct amount above it
    D. write a new check

11. Which one of the following BEST describes the usual arrangement of a tickler file?
    A. Alphabetical
    B. Chronological
    C. Numerical
    D. Geographical

11.____

12. Which one of the following is the LEAST desirable filing practice?
    A. Using staples to keep papers together
    B. Filing all material without regard to date
    C. Keeping a record of all materials removed from the files
    D. Writing filing instructions on each paper prior to filing

12.____

13. Assume that one of your duties is to keep records of the office supplies used by your unit for the purpose of ordering new supplies when the old supplies run out.
    The information that will be of MOST help in letting you know when to reorder supplies is the
    A. quantity issued
    B. quantity received
    C. quantity on hand
    D. stock number

13.____

Questions 14-19.

DIRECTIONS: Questions 14 through 19 consist of sets of names and addresses. In each question, the name and address in Column II should be an exact copy of the name and address in Column I. If there is
a mistake *only* in the name, mark your answer A;
a mistake *only* in the address, mark your answer B;
a mistake in *both* name and address, mark your answer C;
no mistake in either name or address, mark your answer D.

SAMPLE QUESTION

Column I
Michael Filbert
456 Reade Street
New York, N.Y. 10013

Column II
Michael Filbert
645 Reade Street
New York, N.Y. 10013

Since there is a mistake only in the address (the street number should be 456 instead of 645), the answer to the sample question is B.

COLUMN I

COLUMN II

14. Esta Wong
    141 West 68 St.
    New York, N.Y. 10023

    Esta Wang
    141 West 68 St.
    New York,, N.Y. 10023

14.____

15. Dr. Alberto Grosso
    3475 12th Avenue
    Brooklyn, N.Y. 11218

    Dr. Alberto Grosso
    3475 12th Avenue
    Brooklyn, N.Y. 11218

15.____

	Column I	Column II	

16. Mrs. Ruth Bortlas
    482 Theresa Ct.
    Far Rockaway, N.Y. 11691

    Ms. Ruth Bortlas
    482 Theresa Ct.
    Far Rockaway, N.Y. 11169

    16.____

17. Mr. and Mrs. Howard Fox
    2301 Sedgwick Avenue
    Bronx, N.Y. 10468

    Mr. and Mrs. Howard Fox
    231 Sedgwick Ave.
    Bronx, N.Y. 10458

    17.____

18. Miss Marjorie Black
    223 East 23 Street
    New York, N.Y. 10010

    Miss Margorie Black
    223 East 23 Street
    New York, N.Y. 10010

    18.____

19. Michelle Herman
    806 Valley Rd.
    Old Tappan, N.J. 07675

    Michelle Hermann
    806 Valley Dr.
    Old Tappan, N.J. 07675

    19.____

Questions 20-25.

DIRECTIONS: Questions 20 through 25 are to be answered SOLELY on the basis of the information in the following passage.

Basic to every office is the need for proper lighting. Inadequate lighting is a familiar cause of fatigue and serves to create a somewhat dismal atmosphere in the office. One requirement of proper lighting is that it be of an appropriate intensity. Intensity is measured in foot-candles. According to the Illuminating Engineering Society of New York, for casual seeing tasks such as in reception rooms, inactive file rooms, and other service areas, it is recommended that the amount of light be 30 foot-candles. For ordinary seeing tasks such as reading and work in active file rooms and in mail rooms, the recommended lighting is 100 foot-candles. For very difficult seeing tasks such as accounting, transcribing, and business machine use, the recommended lighting is 150 foot-candles.

Lighting intensity is only one requirement. Shadows and glare are to be avoided. For example, the larger the proportion of a ceiling filled with lighting units, the more glare-free and comfortable the lighting will be. Natural lighting from windows is not too dependable because on dark wintry days, windows yield little usable light, and on sunny afternoons, the glare from windows may be very distracting. Desks should not face the windows. Finally, the main lighting source ought to be overhead and to the left of the user.

20. According to the above passage, insufficient light in the office may cause
    A. glare B. shadows C. tiredness D. distraction

    20.____

21. Based on the above passage, which of the following must be considered when planning lighting arrangements?
    The
    A. amount of natural light present
    B. amount of work to be done
    C. level of difficulty of work to be done
    D. type of activity to be carried out

    21.____

5 (#1)

22. It can be inferred from the above passage that a well-coordinated lighting scheme is LIKELY to result in
    A. greater employee productivity
    B. elimination of light reflection
    C. lower lighting cost
    D. more use of natural light

23. Of the following, the BEST title for the above passage is
    A. Characteristics of Light
    B. Light Measurement Devices
    C. Factors to Consider When Planning Lighting Systems
    D. Comfort vs. Cost When Devising Lighting Arrangements

24. According to the above passage, a foot-candle is a measurement of the
    A. number of bulbs used
    B. strength of the light
    C. contrast between glare and shadow
    D. proportion of the ceiling filled with lighting units

25. According to the above passage, the number of foot-candles of light that would be needed to copy figures onto a payroll is _____ foot-candles.
    A. less than 30   B. 30   C. 100   D. 150

KEY (CORRECT ANSWERS)

1.	B		11.	B
2.	B		12.	B
3.	B		13.	C
4.	A		14.	A
5.	B		15.	D
6.	A		16.	C
7.	A		17.	B
8.	D		18.	A
9.	B		19.	C
10.	D		20.	C

21. D
22. A
23. C
24. B
25. D

TEST 2

DIRECTIONS: Each question or incomplete statement is followed by several suggested answers or completions. Select the one that BEST answers the question or completes the statement. *PRINT THE LETTER OF THE CORRECT ANSWER IN THE SPACE AT THE RIGHT.*

1. Assume that a supervisor has three subordinates who perform clerical tasks. One of the employees retires and is replaced by someone who is transferred from another unit in the agency. The transferred employee tells the supervisor that she has worked as a clerical employee for two years and understands clerical operations quite well. The supervisor then assigns the transferred employee to a desk, tells the employee to begin working, and returns to his own desk.
The supervisor's action in this situation is
    A. *proper;* experienced clerical employees do not require training when they are transferred to new assignments
    B. *improper;* before the supervisor returns to his desk, he should tell the other two subordinates to watch the transferred employee perform the work
    C. *proper;* if the transferred employee makes any mistakes, she will bring them to the supervisor's attention
    D. *improper;* the supervisor should find out what clerical tasks the transferred employee has performed and give her instruction in those which are new or different

1.____

2. Assume that you are falling behind in completing your work assignments and you believe that your workload is too heavy.
Of the following, the BEST course of action for you to take FIRST is to
    A. discuss the problem with your supervisor
    B. decide which of your assignments can be postponed
    C. try to get some of your co-workers to help you out
    D. plan to take some of the work home with you in order to catch up

2.____

3. Suppose that one of the clerks under your supervision is filling in monthly personnel forms. She asks you to explain a particular personnel regulation which is related to various items on the forms. You are not thoroughly familiar with the regulation.
Of the following responses you may make, the one which will gain the MOST respect from the clerk and which is generally the MOST advisable is to
    A. tell the clerk to do the best she can and that you will check her work later
    B. inform the clerk that you are not sure of a correct explanation but suggest a procedure for her to follow
    C. give the clerk a suitable interpretation so that she will think you are familiar with all regulations
    D. tell the clerk that you will have to read the regulation more thoroughly before you can give her an explanation

3.____

4. Charging out records until a specified due date, with prompt follow-up if they are not returned, is a 4._____
   A. *good* idea; it may prevent the records from being kept needlessly on someone's desk for long periods of time
   B. *good* idea; it will indicate the extent of your authority to other departments
   C. *poor* idea; the person borrowing the material may make an error because of the pressure put upon him to return the records
   D. *poor* idea; other departments will feel that you do not trust them with the records and they will be resentful

Questions 5-9.

DIRECTIONS: Questions 5 through 9 consist of three lines of code letters and numbers. The numbers on each line should correspond with the code letters on the same line in accordance with the table below.

Code Letter	P	L	I	J	B	O	H	U	C	G
Corresponding Letter	0	1	2	3	4	5	6	7	8	9

On some of the lines, an error exists in the coding. Compare the letters and numbers in each question carefully. If you find an error or errors on
only one of the lines in the question, mark your answer A;
any two lines in the question, mark your answer B;
all three lines in the question, mark your answer C;
none of the lines in the question, mark your answer D.

SAMPLE QUESTION
JHOILCP   3652180
BICLGUP   4286970
UCIBHLJ   5824613

In the above sample, the first line is correct since each code letter listed has the correct corresponding number. On the second line, an error exists because code letter L should have the number 1 instead of the number 6. On the third line, an error exists because the code letter U should have the number 7 instead of the number 5. Since there are errors on two of the three lines, the correct answer is B.

5. BULJCIP   4713920 5._____
    HIGPOUL   6290571
    OCUHJJBI   5876342

6. CUBLOIJ   8741023 6._____
    LCLGCLB   1818914
    JPUHIOC   3076158

7. OIJGCBPO   52398405 7._____
    UHPBLIOP   76041250
    CLUIPGPC   81720908

8.	BPCOUOJI	40875732	8._____
	UOHCIPLB	75682014	
	GLHUUCBJ	92677843	

9.	HOIOHJLH	65256361	9._____
	IOJJHHBP	25536640	
	OJHBJOPI	53642502	

Questions 10-13.

DIRECTIONS: Questions 10 through 13 are to be answered SOLELY on the basis of the information given in the following passage.

The mental attitude of the employee toward safety is exceedingly important in preventing accidents. All efforts designed to keep safety on the employee's mind and to keep accident prevention a live subject in the office will help substantially in a safety program. Although it may seem strange, it is common for people to be careless. Therefore, safety education is a continuous process.

Safety rules should be explained, and the reasons for their rigid enforcement should be given to employees. Telling employees to be careful or giving similar general safety warnings and slogans is probably of little value. Employees should be informed of basic safety fundamentals. This can be done through staff meetings, informal suggestions to employees, movies, and safety instruction cards. Safety instruction cards provide the employees with specific suggestions about safety and serve as a series of timely reminder helping to keep safety on the minds of employees. Pictures, posters, and cartoon sketches on bulletin boards that are located in areas continually used by employees arouse the employees' interest in safety. It is usually good to supplement this type of safety promotion with intensive individual follow-up.

10. The above passage implies that the LEAST effective of the following safety measures is
    A. rigid enforcement of safety rules
    B. getting employees to think in terms of safety
    C. elimination of unsafe conditions in the office
    D. telling employees to stay alert at all times

10._____

11. The reason given by the passage for maintaining ongoing safety education is that
    A. people are often careless
    B. office tasks are often dangerous
    C. the value of safety slogans increases with repetition
    D. safety rules change frequently

11._____

12. Which one of the following safety aids is MOST likely to be preferred by the passage? A
    A. cartoon of a man tripping over a carton and yelling, *Keep aisles clear!*
    B. poster with a large number one and a caption saying, *Safety First*

12._____

C. photograph of a very neatly arranged office
D. large sign with the word THINK in capital letters

13. Of the following, the BEST title for the above passage is
    A. Basic Safety Fundamentals
    B. Enforcing Safety Among Careless Employees
    C. Attitudes Toward Safety
    D. Making Employees Aware of Safety

Questions 14-21.

DIRECTIONS: Questions 14 through 21 are to be answered SOLELY on the basis of the information and chart given below.

The following chart shows expenses in five selected categories for a one-year period, expressed as percentages of these same expenses during the previous year. The chart compares two different offices. In Office T (represented by ▓▓▓▓), a cost reduction program has been tested for the past year. The other office, Office Q (represented by ////), served as a control, in that no special effort was made to reduce costs during the past year.

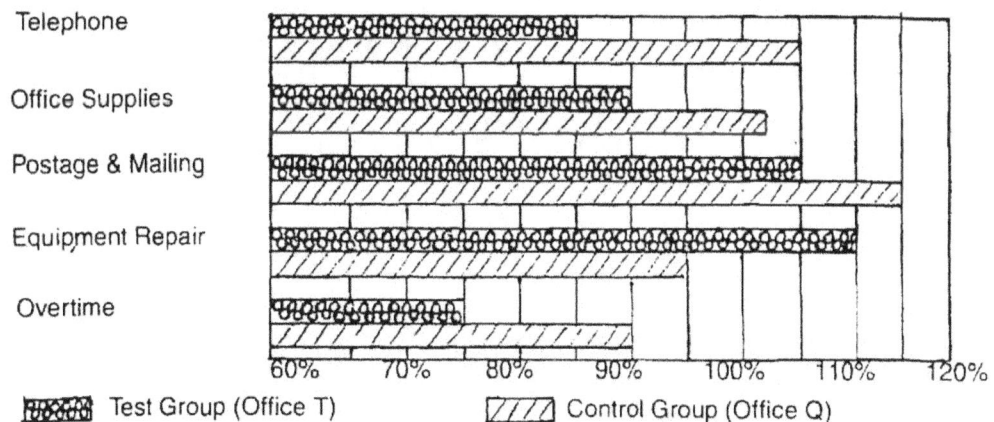

RESULTS OF OFFICE COST REDUCTION PROGRAM
Expenses of Test and Control Groups for 2020
Expressed as Percentages of Same Expenses for 2019

14. In Office T, which category of expense showed the greatest percentage REDUCTION from 2019 to 2020?
    A. Telephone
    B. Office Supplies
    C. Postage & Mailing
    D. Overtime

15. In which expense category did Office T show the BEST results in percentage terms when compared to Office Q?
    A. Telephone
    B. Office Supplies
    C. Postage & Mailing
    D. Overtime

16. According to the above chart, the cost reduction program was LEAST effective for the expense category of
    A. Office Supplies
    B. Postage & Mailing
    C. Equipment Repair
    D. Overtime

17. Office T's telephone costs went down during 2020 by approximately how many percentage points?
    A. 15
    B. 20
    C. 85
    D. 104

18. Which of the following changes occurred in expenses for Office Supplies in Office Q in the year 2020 as compared with the year 2019?
    They
    A. increased by more than 100%
    B. remained the same
    C. decreased by a few percentage points
    D. increased by a few percentage points

19. For which of the following expense categories do the results in Office T and the results in Office Q differ MOST NEARLYY by 10 percentage points?
    A. Telephone
    B. Postage & Mailing
    C. Equipment Repair
    D. Overtime

20. In which expense category did Office Q's costs show the GREATEST percentage increase in 2020?
    A. Telephone
    B. Office Supplies
    C. Postage & Mailing
    D. Equipment Repair

21. In Office T, by approximately what percentage did overtime expense change during the past year? It
    A. *increased* by 15%
    B. *increased* by 75%
    C. *decreased* by 10%
    D. *decreased* by 25%

22. In a particular agency, there were 160 accidents in 2017. Of these accidents, 75% were due to unsafe acts and the rest were due to unsafe conditions. In the following year, a special safety program was established. The number of accidents in 2019 due to unsafe acts was reduced to 35% of what it had been in 2017.
    How many accidents due to unsafe acts were there in 2019?
    A. 20
    B. 36
    C. 42
    D. 56

23. At the end of every month, the petty cash fund of Agency A is reimbursed for payments made from the fund during the month. During the month of February, the amounts paid from the fund were entered on receipts as follows: 10 bus fares of $3.50 each and one taxi fare of $35.00. At the end of the month, the money left in the fund was in the following denominations: 15 ten-dollar bills, 10 one-dollar bills, 40 quarters, and 100 dimes.
    If the petty cash fund is reduced by 20% for the following month, how much money will there be available in the petty cash fund for March?
    A. $110.00
    B. $200.00
    C. $215.00
    D. $250.00

6 (#2)

24. The one of the following records which it would be MOST advisable to keep in alphabetical order is a
    A. continuous listing of phone messages, including time and caller, for your supervisor
    B. listing of individuals currently employed by your agency in a particular title
    C. record of purchases paid for by the petty cash fund
    D. dated record of employees who have borrowed material from the files in your office

25. Assume that you have been asked to copy by hand a column of numbers with two decimal places from one record to another. Each number consists of three, four, and five digits.
    In order to copy them quickly and accurately, you should copy
    A. each number exactly, making sure that the column of digits farthest to the right is in a straight line and all other columns are lined up
    B. the column of digits farthest to the right and then copy the next column of digits moving from right to left
    C. the column of digits farthest to the left and then copy the next column of digits moving from left to right
    D. the digits to the right of each decimal point and then copy the digits to the left of each decimal point

KEY (CORRECT ANSWERS)

1.	D		11.	A
2.	A		12.	A
3.	D		13.	D
4.	A		14.	D
5.	A		15.	A
6.	C		16.	C
7.	D		17.	A
8.	B		18.	D
9.	C		19.	B
10.	D		20.	C

21. D
22. C
23. B
24. B
25. A

EXAMINATION SECTION
TEST 1

DIRECTIONS: Each question or incomplete statement is followed by several suggested answers or completions. Select the one that BEST answers the question or completes the statement. *PRINT THE LETTER OF THE CORRECT ANSWER IN THE SPACE AT THE RIGHT.*

Questions 1-10.

WORD MEANING

DIRECTIONS: Each question from 1 to 10 contains a word in capitals followed by four suggested meanings of the word. For each question, choose the best meaning. *PRINT THE LETTER OF THE CORRECT ANSWER IN THE SPACE AT THE RIGHT.*

1. ACCURATE
   A. correct   B. useful   C. afraid   D. careless

2. ALTER
   A. copy   B. change   C. report   D. agree

3. DOCUMENT
   A. outline   B. agreement   C. blueprint   D. record

4. INDICATE
   A. listen   B. show   C. guess   D. try

5. INVENTORY
   A. custom   B. discovery   C. warning   D. list

6. ISSUE
   A. annoy   B. use up   C. give out   D. gain

7. NOTIFY
   A. inform   B. promise   C. approve   D. strengthen

8. ROUTINE
   A. path   B. mistake   C. habit   D. journey

9. TERMINATE
   A. rest   B. start   C. deny   D. end

10. TRANSMIT
    A. put in   B. send   C. stop   D. go across

Questions 11-15.

READING COMPREHENSION

DIRECTIONS: Questions 11 through 15 test how well you understand what you read. It will be necessary for you to read carefully because your answers to these questions should be based ONLY on the information given in the following paragraphs.

The recipient gains an impression of a typewritten letter before he begins to read the message. Pastors which provide for a good first impression include margins and spacing that are visually pleasing, formal parts of the letter which are correctly placed according to the style of the letter, copy which is free of obvious erasures and over-strikes, and transcript that is even and clear. The problem for the typist is that of how to produce that first, positive impression of her work.

There are several general rules which a typist can follow when she wishes to prepare a properly spaced letter on a sheet of letter-head. Ordinarily, the width of a letter should not be less than four inches nor more than six inches. The side margins should also have a desirable relation to the bottom margin and the space between the letterhead and the body of the letter. Usually the most appealing arrangement is when the side margins are even and the bottom margin is slightly wider than the side margins. In some offices, however, standard line length is used for all business letters, and the secretary then varies the spacing between the date line and the inside address according to the length of the letter.

11. The BEST title for the above paragraphs would be: 11.____

    A. Writing Office Letters
    B. Making Good First Impressions
    C. Judging Well-Typed Letters
    D. Good Placing and Spacing for Office Letters

12. According to the above paragraphs, which of the following might be considered the way in which people very quickly judge the quality of work which has been typed? By 12.____

    A. measuring the margins to see if they are correct
    B. looking at the spacing and cleanliness of the typescript
    C. scanning the body of the letter for meaning
    D. reading the date line and address for errors

13. What, according to the above paragraphs, would be definitely UNDESIRABLE as the average line length of a typed letter? 13.____

    A. 4"   B. 5"   C. 6"   D. 7"

14. According to the above paragraphs, when the line length is kept standard, the secretary 14.____

    A. does not have to vary the spacing at all since this also is standard
    B. adjusts the spacing between the date line and inside address for different lengths of letters
    C. uses the longest line as a guideline for spacing between the date line and inside address
    D. varies the number of spaces between the lines

15. According to the above paragraphs, side margins are MOST pleasing when they 15._____
    A. are even and somewhat smaller than the bottom margin
    B. are slightly wider than the bottom margin
    C. vary with the length of the letter
    D. are figured independently from the letterhead and the body of the letter

Questions 16-20.

CODING

DIRECTIONS:

Name of Applicant	H	A	N	G	S	B	R	U	K	E
Test Code	c	o	m	p	l	e	x	i	t	y
File Number	0	1	2	3	4	5	6	7	8	9

Assume that each of the above capital letters is the first letter of the name of an Applicant, that the small letter directly beneath each capital letter is the test code for the Applicant, and that the number directly beneath each code letter is the file number for the Applicant.

In each of the following Questions 16 through 20, the test code letters and the file numbers in Columns 2 and 3 should correspond to the capital letters in Column 1. For each question, look at each column carefully and mark your answer as follows:

If there is an error only in Column 2, mark your answer A.
If there is an error only in Column 3, mark your answer B.
If there is an error in both Columns 2 and 3, mark your answer C.
If both Columns 2 and 3 are correct, mark your answer D.

The following sample question is given to help you understand the procedure.

SAMPLE QUESTION

Column 1	Column 2	Column 3
AKEHN	otyci	18902

In Column 2, the final test code letter *i.* should be *m*. Column 3 is correctly coded to Column 1. Since there is an error only in Column 2, the answer is A.

	Column 1	Column 2	Column 3	
16.	NEKKU	mytti	29987	16._____
17.	KRAEB	txyle	86095	17._____
18.	ENAUK	ymoit	92178	18._____
19.	REANA	xeomo	69121	19._____
20.	EKHSE	ytcxy	97049	20._____

Questions 21-30.

ARITHMETICAL REASONING

21. If a secretary answered 28 phone calls and typed the addresses for 112 credit statements in one morning, what is the ratio of phone calls answered to credit statements typed for that period of time?

    A. 1:4   B. 1:7   C. 2:3   D. 3:5

22. According to a suggested filing system, no more than 10 folders should be filed behind any one file guide and from 15 to 25 file guides should be used in each file drawer for easy finding and filing.
    The maximum number of folders that a five-drawer file cabinet can hold to allow easy finding and filing is

    A. 550   B. 750   C. 1,100   D. 1,250

23. An employee had a starting salary of $25,804. He received a salary increase at the end of each year, and at the end of the seventh year his salary was $33,476.
    What was his average annual increase in salary over these seven years?

    A. $1,020   B. $1,076   C. $1,096   D. $1,144

24. The 55 typists and 28 senior clerks in a certain city agency were paid a total of $1,943,200 in salaries last year.
    If the average annual salary of a typist was $22,400 the average annual salary of a senior clerk was

    A. $25,400   B. $26,600   C. $26,800   D. $27,000

25. A typist has been given a three page report to type. She has finished typing the first two pages. The first page has 283 words, and the second page has 366 words.
    If the total report consists of 954 words, how many words will she have to type on the third page of the report?

    A. 202   B. 287   C. 305   D. 313

26. In one day, Clerk A processed 30% more forms than Clerk B, and Clerk C processed li times as many forms as Clerk A. If Clerk B processed 40 forms, how many more forms were processed by Clerk C than Clerk B?

    A. 12   B. 13   C. 21   D. 25

27. A clerk who earns a gross salary of $452 every two weeks has the following deductions taken from her paycheck:
    15% for City, State, Federal taxes; 2 1/2% for Social Security; $1.30 for health insurance; and $6.00 for union dues. The amount of her take-home pay is

    A. $256.20   B. $312.40   C. $331.60   D. $365.60

28. In 2005, a city agency spent $2,000 to buy pencils at a cost of $5.00 a dozen.
    If the agency used 3/4 of these pencils in 2005 and used the same number of pencils in 2006, how many more pencils did it have to buy to have enough pencils for all of 2006?

    A. 1,200   B. 2,400   C. 3,600   D. 4,800

29. A clerk who worked in Agency X earned the following salaries: $20,140 the first year, $21,000 the second year, and $21,920 the third year. Another clerk who worked in Agency Y for three years earned $21,100 a year for two years and $21,448 the third year. The difference between the average salaries received by both clerks over a three-year period is

    A. $196 B. $204 C. $348 D. $564

    29.____

30. An employee who works over 40 hours in any week receives overtime payment for the extra hours at time and one-half (1 1/2 times) his hourly rate of pay. An employee who earns $13.60 an hour works a total of 45 hours during a certain week.
    His total pay for that week would be

    A. $564.40 B. $612.00 C. $646.00 D. $812.00

    30.____

Questions 31-35.

RELATED INFORMATION

31. To tell a newly-employed clerk to fill a top drawer of a four-drawer cabinet with heavy folders which will be often used and to keep lower drawers only partly filled is

    A. *good,* because a tall person would have to bend unnecessarily if he had to use a lower drawer
    B. *bad,* because the file cabinet may tip over when the top drawer is opened
    C. *good,* because it is the most easily reachable drawer for the average person
    D. *bad,* because a person bending down at another drawer may accidentally bang his head on the bottom of the drawer when he straightens up

    31.____

32. If a senior typist or senior clerk has requisitioned a *ream* of paper in order to duplicate a single page office announcement, how many announcements can be printed from the one package of paper?

    A. 200 B. 500 C. 700 D. 1,000

    32.____

33. Your supervisor has asked you to locate a telephone number for an attorney named Jones, whose office is located at 311 Broadway, and whose name is not already listed in your files.
    The BEST method for finding the number would be for you to

    A. call the information operator and have her get it for you
    B. look in the alphabetical directory (white pages) under the name Jones at 311 Broadway
    C. refer to the heading Attorney in the yellow pages for the name Jones at 311 Broadway
    D. ask your supervisor who referred her to Mr. Jones, then call that person for the number

    33.____

34. An example of material that should NOT be sent by first class mail is a

    A. email copy of a letter   B. post card
    C. business reply card   D. large catalogue

    34.____

35. In the operations of a government agency, a voucher is ORDINARILY used to   35._____
    A. refer someone to the agency for a position or assignment
    B. certify that an agency's records of financial trans-actions are accurate
    C. order payment from agency funds of a stated amount to an individual
    D. enter a statement of official opinion in the records of the agency

Questions 36-40.

ENGLISH USAGE

DIRECTIONS: Each question from 36 through 40 contains a sentence. Read each sentence carefully to decide whether it is correct. Then, in the space at the right, mark your answer:

(A) if the sentence is incorrect because of bad grammar or sentence structure

(B) if the sentence is incorrect because of bad punctuation

(C) if the sentence is incorrect because of bad capitalization

(D) if the sentence is correct

Each incorrect sentence has only one type of error. Consider a sentence correct if it has no errors, although there may be other correct ways of saying the same thing.

SAMPLE QUESTION I: One of our clerks were promoted yesterday.

The subject of this sentence is *one*, so the verb should be *was promoted* instead of *were promoted*. Since the sentence is incorrect because of bad grammar, the answer to Sample Question I is (A).

SAMPLE QUESTION II: Between you and me, I would prefer not going there.

Since this sentence is correct, the answer to Sample Question II is (D).

36. The National alliance of Businessmen is trying to persuade private businesses to hire youth in the summertime.   36._____

37. The supervisor who is on vacation, is in charge of processing vouchers.   37._____

38. The activity of the committee at its conferences is always stimulating.   38._____

39. After checking the addresses again, the letters went to the mailroom.   39._____

40. The director, as well as the employees, are interested in sharing the dividends.   40._____

Questions 41-45.

FILING

DIRECTIONS: Each question from 41 through 45 contains four names. For each question, choose the name that should be FIRST if the four names are to be arranged in alphabetical order in accordance with the Rules for Alphabetical Filing given below. Read these rules carefully. Then, for each question, indicate in the space at the right the letter before the name that should be FIRST in alphabetical order.

RULES FOR ALPHABETICAL FILING

Names of People

(1) The names of people are filed in strict alphabetical order, first according to the last name, then according to first name or initial, and finally according to middle name or initial. FOR EXAMPLE: George Allen comes before Edward Bell, and Leonard P. Reston comes before Lucille B. Reston.

(2) When last names are the same, FOR EXAMPLE, A. Green and Agnes Green, the one with the initial comes before the one with the name written out when the first initials are identical.

(3) When first and last names are alike and the middle name is given, FOR EXAMPLE, John David Doe and John Devoe Doe, the names should be filed in the alphabetical order of the middle names.

(4) When first and last names are the same, a name without a middle initial comes before one with a middle name or initial. FOR EXAMPLE, John Doe comes before both John A. Doe and John Alan Doe.

(5) When first and last names are the same, a name with a middle initial comes before one with a middle name beginning with the same initial. FOR EXAMPLE: Jack R. Hertz comes before Jack Richard Hertz.

(6) Prefixes such as De, O', Mac, Mc, and Van are filed as written and are treated as part of the names to which they are connected. FOR EXAMPLE: Robert O'Dea is filed before David Olsen.

(7) Abbreviated names are treated as if they were spelled out. FOR EXAMPLE: Chas. is filed as Charles and Thos. is filed as Thomas.

(8) Titles and designations such as Dr., Mr., and Prof, are disregarded in filing.

Names of Organizations

(1) The names of business organizations are filed according to the order in which each word in the name appears. When an organization name bears the name of a person, it is filed according to the rules for filing names of people as given above. FOR EXAMPLE: William Smith Service Co. comes before Television Distributors, Inc.

(2) Where bureau, board, office, or department appears as the first part of the title of a governmental agency, that agency should be filed under the word in the title expressing the chief function of the agency. FOR EXAMPLE: Bureau of the Budget would be filed as if written Budget, (Bureau of the). The Department of Personnel would be filed as if written Personnel, (Department of).

(3) When the following words are part of an organization, they are disregarded: the, of, and.

(4) When there are numbers in a name, they are treated as if they were spelled out. FOR EXAMPLE: 10th Street Bootery is filed as Tenth Street Bootery.

SAMPLE QUESTION:
- A. Jane Earl (2)
- B. James A. Earle (4)
- C. James Earl (1)
- D. J. Earle (3)

The numbers in parentheses show the proper alphabetical order in which these names should be filed. Since the name that should be filed FIRST is James Earl, the answer to the Sample Question is (C).

41.
- A. Majorca Leather Goods
- B. Robert Maiorca and Sons
- C. Maintenance Management Corp.
- D. Majestic Carpet Mills

42.
- A. Municipal Telephone Service
- B. Municipal Reference Library
- C. Municipal Credit Union
- D. Municipal Broadcasting System

43.
- A. Robert B. Pierce
- B. R. Bruce Pierce
- C. Ronald Pierce
- D. Robert Bruce Pierce

44.
- A. Four Seasons Sports Club
- B. 14th. St. Shopping Center
- C. Forty Thieves Restaurant
- D. 42nd St. Theaters

45.
- A. Franco Franceschini
- B. Amos Franchini
- C. Sandra Franceschia
- D. Lilie Franchinesca

Questions 46-50.

SPELLING

DIRECTIONS: In each question, one of the words is misspelled. Select the letter of the misspelled word. *PRINT THE LETTER OF THE CORRECT ANSWER IN THE SPACE AT THE RIGHT.*

46.
- A. option
- B. extradite
- C. comparitive
- D. jealousy

47.
- A. handicaped
- B. assurance
- C. sympathy
- D. speech

48. A. recommend   B. carraige   48.____
    C. disapprove   D. independent

49. A. ingenuity   B. tenet (opinion) 49.____
    C. uncanny   D. intrigueing

50. A. arduous   B. hideous   50.____
    C. iervant   D. companies

KEY (CORRECT ANSWERS)

1. A	11. D	21. A	31. B	41. C
2. B	12. B	22. D	32. B	42. D
3. D	13. D	23. C	33. C	43. B
4. B	14. B	24. A	34. D	44. D
5. D	15. A	25. C	35. C	45. C
6. C	16. B	26. D	36. C	46. C
7. A	17. C	27. D	37. B	47. A
8. C	18. D	28. B	38. D	48. B
9. D	19. A	29. A	39. A	49. D
10. B	20. C	30. C	40. A	50. C'

EXAMINATION SECTION
TEST 1

DIRECTIONS: Each question or incomplete statement is followed by several suggested answers or completions. Select the one that BEST answers the question or completes the statement. *PRINT THE LETTER OF THE CORRECT ANSWER IN THE SPACE AT THE RIGHT.*

1. In considering a new word processing system for a regional office, which of the following would MOST likely be the MOST important consideration in making a decision?   1.____

    A. Ease of operation
    B. Friendliness of service technicians
    C. Availability of service technicians
    D. Capacity of the system to meet the unit's word processing needs

2. Your supervisor is out of town for several days and has asked you to act as supervisor in his absence. An employee in the unit comes to you and complains that the supervisor has been dividing the workload unfairly.
Of the following, the MOST appropriate action for you to take is   2.____

    A. defend the actions of your supervisor
    B. encourage the employee to file a grievance
    C. listen to the employee attentively
    D. explain to the employee that you have no authority to handle the situation

3. A principal stenographer still on probation is instructed to supervise and coordinate the completion of a large word processing project. Her supervisor asks her how long she thinks the project will take. The principal stenographer gives her supervisor an estimate that is two days longer than she actually thinks the project will take to complete. The project is completed two days earlier, and the principal stenographer is congratulated by her supervisor for her efforts.
In purposely overestimating the time required to complete the project, the principal stenographer showed   3.____

    A. *good* judgment because it helped her appear very efficient
    B. *good* judgment because it helps keep unrealistic supervisors from expecting too much
    C. *poor* judgment because plans and schedules of other components of the project may have been based on her false estimate
    D. *poor* judgment because she should have used the extra time to further check and, proofread the work

4. Which of the following would MOST likely be the MOST important in providing support to one's supervisor?   4.____

    A. Screening annoying phone calls
    B. Reviewing and forwarding articles and publications that may be of interest to your supervisor
    C. Correctly transmitting instructions from the supervisor to appropriate staff members
    D. Reviewing outgoing correspondence for proper grammatical usage and clarity

5. While you are on the telephone answering a question about your agency, a visitor comes to your desk and starts to ask you a question. There is no emergency or urgency in either situation, that of the phone call or that of answering the visitor's question.
   In this case, you should

   A. excuse yourself to the person on the telephone and tell the visitor that you will be with him or her as soon as you have finished on the phone
   B. explain to the person on the phone that you have a visitor and must shorten the conversation
   C. continue to talk with the person on the phone while looking up occasionally at the visitor to let him or her know that you know he or she is there
   D. continue to talk with the person on the telephone until you are finished and then let the visitor know that you're sorry to have kept him or her waiting

6. Your supervisor is out of town on vacation for one week, and asks you to act as supervisor in her absence. The second day she is gone a very important, complex budgetary form, which must be responded to in ten days, arrives in your unit.
   Of the following, it would be BEST if you

   A. filled out the form and submitted it as soon as possible
   B. read the form over, did any time-consuming research that might be needed, and then gave the uncompleted form to your supervisor as soon as she returned
   C. asked for help from your supervisor's supervisor in completing the form
   D. tried to contact your supervisor for advice

7. Of the following, which would MOST likely be of the highest priority?
   The typing of

   A. a grant proposal due next week
   B. new addresses onto a mailing list for a future mailing
   C. a payroll form for a new employee that needs to be submitted immediately
   D. a memorandum from the Commissioner to all employees regarding new procedures

8. Your office is moving to a new location.
   Of the following, it would be MOST important to ensure that

   A. others will know your office's new address and phone number
   B. the new office space is comfortable
   C. your supervisor is happy with his or her new office space
   D. the move itself goes smoothly

9. Of the following, which would generally be considered the LEAST desirable?

   A. Accidentally disconnecting an executive from an important phone call
   B. Ordering the wrong back-up part for a copying machine
   C. Misplacing several hundred dollars worth of personal checks payable to your department
   D. Misplacing a memorandum that needs to be typed

10. Your supervisor has told you not to let anyone disturb her for the rest of the morning unless absolutely necessary because she has some urgent work to complete. The department head telephones and asks to speak to her.
    The BEST course of action for you to take is to

    A. ask the department head if he or she can leave a message
    B. ask your supervisor if she can take the call
    C. tell the department head that your supervisor is out
    D. let your supervisor know that her instructions have put you in a difficult position

11. Which of the following would be MOST likely to contribute to efficiency in the operation of an office?

    A. A new computer system is instituted in an office.
    B. The employees are paid well.
    C. Procedures and practices are studied for any redundant operations.
    D. A supervisor delegates work.

12. You are at work at your desk on a special project when a visitor approaches you. You cannot interrupt your work to take care of this person.
    Of the following, the BEST and MOST courteous way of handling this situation is to

    A. avoid looking up from your work until you are finished with what you are doing
    B. tell the visitor that you will not be able to assist him or her for quite some time
    C. refer the individual to another employee who can take care of him or her right away
    D. chat with the individual while you continue to work

13. Which of the following would MOST likely be of the highest priority?
    A(n)

    A. annual report due next month
    B. irate member of the public who is standing at your desk
    C. important financial report requested by the Commissioner
    D. memorandum to all employees outlining very important new policy needs to be typed and distributed immediately

14. Someone uses *special pull* to obtain the services of your unit at the last minute. You and the four employees you supervise have done everything you could do to provide good service, and you feel things have gone very well. The client is not pleased, however, and enters your office and begins screaming at you and the other employees present.
    Of the following, it would be BEST if you

    A. ignored the person
    B. tried to calm the person down
    C. asked the person to leave the office
    D. called your supervisor in to help handle the situation

15. Your supervisor is on vacation for two weeks, and you have been asked to fill in for her. Your office is very busy, and there is a strict procedure for filling requests. Leslie from Unit X wants something completed immediately. You don't feel this is possible or reasonable, and politely explain why to Leslie. Leslie becomes very angry and says that she will complain to your supervisor about your uncooperative behavior as soon as your supervisor returns.
Of the following, it would be BEST if you

    A. filled Leslie's request
    B. reported Leslie to her supervisor
    C. complained to your supervisor about the situation as soon as she returned
    D. stood by your decision once you determined it was correct

KEY (CORRECT ANSWERS)

1. D	6. B	11. C
2. C	7. C	12. C
3. C	8. A	13. B
4. C	9. C	14. B
5. A	10. B	15. D

EXAMINATION SECTION
TEST 1

DIRECTIONS: Each question or incomplete statement is followed by several suggested answers or completions. Select the one that BEST answers the question or completes the statement. *PRINT THE LETTER OF THE CORRECT ANSWER IN THE SPACE AT THE RIGHT.*

Questions 1-50.

DIRECTIONS: One word in each of Questions 1 through 50 is MISSPELLED. Indicate the letter of the MISSPELLED word in the space at the right.

1. A. statute B. stationary C. staturesque D. stature   1._____

2. A. practicible B. practical C. particle D. reticule   2._____

3. A. plague B. plaque C. ague D. aigrete   3._____

4. A. theology B. idealogy C. psychology D. philology   4._____

5. A. dilema B. stamina C. feminine C. strychnine   5._____

6. A. deceit B. benefit C. grieve D. hienous   6._____

7. A. commensurable B. measurable C. duteable C. salable   7._____

8. A. homogeneous B. heterogeneous C. advantageous D. religeous   8._____

9. A. criticize B. dramatise C. exorcise D. exercise   9._____

10. A. maintain B. maintainance C. sustain D. sustenance   10._____

11. A. portend B. portentious C. pretend D. pretentious   11._____

12. A. prophesize B. prophesies C. farinaceous D. spaceous   12._____

13. A. choose B. chose C. choosen D. chasten   13._____

14. A. censure B. censorious C. pleasure D. pleasurible   14._____

15. A. cover B. coverage C. adder D. adege   15._____

16. A. balloon B. diregible C. direct D. descent   16._____

2 (#1)

17.	A.	whemsy	B.	crazy	C.	flimsy	D.	lazy	17.____
18.	A.	derision	B.	pretention					18.____
	C.	sustention	D.	contention				
19.	A.	question	B.	questionaire					19.____
	A.	legion	B.	legionary				
20.	A.	chattle	B.	cattle	C.	dismantle	D.	kindle	20.____
21.	A.	canal	B.	cannel	C.	chanel	D.	colonel	21.____
22.	A.	hemorrage	B.	storage	C.	manage	D.	foliage	22.____
23.	A.	surgeon	B.	sturgeon	C.	luncheon	D.	stancheon	23.____
24.	A.	facial	B.	physical	C.	fiscle	D.	muscle	24.____
25.	A.	congradulate	B.	percolate					25.____
	C.	major	D.	leisure				
26.	A.	convenience	B.	privilige					26.____
	C.	emerge	D.	immerse				
27.	A.	erasable	B.	inflammable					27.____
	C.	audable	D.	laudable				
28.	A.	final	B.	fines	C.	finis	D.	Finish	28.____
29.	A.	emitted	B.	representative					29.____
	C.	discipline	D.	insistance				
30.	A.	diphthong	B.	rarified	C.	library	D.	recommend	30.____
31.	A.	compel	B.	belligerent					31.____
	C.	successful	D.	sargeant				
32.	A.	dispatch	B.	dispise	C.	dispose	D.	dispute	32.____
33.	A.	administrator	B.	adviser					33.____
	C.	diner	D.	celluler				
34.	A.	ignite	B.	ignision	C.	igneous	D.	ignited	34.____
35.	A.	pallor	B.	ballid	C.	ballet	D.	pallid	35.____
36.	A.	urbane	B.	surburbane					36.____
	C.	interurban	D.	urban				
37.	A.	symtom	B.	serum					37.____
	C.	antiseptic	D.	aromatic				
38.	A.	register	B.	registrar	C.	purser	D.	burser	38.____
39.	A.	athletic	B.	tragedy					39.____
	C.	batallion	D.	sophomore				

40. A. latent   B. godess   C. aisle   D. whose   40.____
41. A. rhyme   B. rhythm   C. thime   D. thine   41.____
42. A. eighth   B. exaggerate   42.____
    C. electoral   D. villain
43. A. statute   B. superintendent   43.____
    C. iresistible   D. colleague
44. A. sieze   B. therefor   C. auxiliary   D. changeable   44.____
45. A. siege   B. knowledge   45.____
    C. lieutenent   D. weird
46. A. acquitted   B. polititian   46.____
    C. professor   D. conqueror
47. A. changeable   B. chargeable   47.____
    C. salable   D. useable
48. A. promissory   B. prisoner   48.____
    C. excellent   D. tyrrany
49. A. comptroller   B. traveled   49.____
    C. accede   D. procede
50. A. Britain   B. Brittainica   50.____
    C. conductor   D. vendor

KEY (CORRECT ANSWERS)

1. C	11. B	21. C	31. D	41. C
2. A	12. D	22. A	32. B	42. C
3. D	13. C	23. D	33. D	43. C
4. B	14. D	24. C	34. B	44. A
5. A	15. D	25. A	35. B	45. C
6. D	16. B	26. B	36. B	46. B
7. C	17. A	27. C	37. A	47. D
8. D	18. B	28. D	38. D	48. D
9. B	19. B	29. D	39. C	49. D
10. B	20. A	30. B	40. B	50. B

4 (#1)

CORRECT SPELLING

1. statuesque
2. practicable
3. aigrette
4. ideology
5. dilemma
6. heinous
7. dutiable
8. religious
9. dramatize
10. maintenance
11. portentous
12. spacious
13. chosen
14. pleasurable
15. adage
16. dirigible
17. whimsey or whimsy
18. pretension
19. questionnaire
20. chattel
21. channel
22. hemorrhage
23. stanchion
24. fiscal
25. congratulate
26. privilege
27. audible
28. Finnish
29. insistence
30. rarefied
31. sergeant
32. despise
33. cellular
34. ignition
35. ballad
36. suburban
37. symptom
38. bursar
39. battalion
40. goddess
41. thyme
42. electoral
43. irresistible
44. seize
45. lieutenant
46. politician
47. usable
48. tyranny
49. proceed
50. Britannica

TEST 2

Questions 1-50.

DIRECTIONS: Select the letter of the word or expression that MOST NEARLY expresses the meaning of the capitalized word in the group.

1. FICTITIOUS 1.____
   - A. turbulent
   - B. anxious
   - C. assumed
   - D. scanty

2. ARDENT 2.____
   - A. fervid
   - B. gay
   - C. savage
   - D. untamed

3. BLATANT 3.____
   - A. insipid
   - B. open
   - C. closed
   - D. clamorous

4. DISTRAIT 4.____
   - A. crooked
   - B. narrow
   - C. broken
   - D. absentminded

5. EQUITABLE 5.____
   - A. unbiased
   - B. unjust
   - C. unreasonable
   - D. unfair

6. EXPEDITE 6.____
   - A. hinder
   - B. harm
   - C. send
   - D. hasten

7. LUCRATIVE 7.____
   - A. painful
   - B. creditable
   - C. preferential
   - D. profitable

8. POSTDATED 8.____
   - A. past date
   - B. future date
   - C. no date
   - D. current date

9. RESOURCES 9.____
   - A. debts
   - B. liabilities
   - C. funds
   - D. losses

10. AGENDA 10.____
    - A. receipt
    - B. agent
    - C. combination
    - D. memoranda

11. DISCRETE 11.____
    - A. careful
    - B. prudent
    - C. truthful
    - D. separate

12. DOGMATIC 12.____
    - A. bovine
    - B. canine
    - C. opinionated
    - D. unprincipled

13. INTREPID
    A. fearful   B. fearless   C. fanciful   D. cowardly

14. TENACITY
    A. firmness   B. sagacity   C. temerity   D. thinness

15. ASEPTIC
    A. antique   B. artistic   C. sterile   D. austere

16. CREDIBLE
    A. believable   B. unbelievable
    C. correct   D. suitable

17. LESSEE
    A. lender   B. giver   C. receiver   D. renter

18. IGNOMINY
    A. illiteracy   B. ill luck
    C. disgrace   D. despair

19. PRODIGAL
    A. wasteful   B. marvelous   C. ominous   D. harmless

20. VOLUBLE
    A. bulky   B. glib   C. desirable   D. malleable

21. JAMB
    A. doorway   B. crowd   C. fruit   D. animal

22. ATOMIC
    A. combustible   B. minute
    C. crystalline   D. ambient

23. ACUMEN
    A. beauty   B. poise
    C. keen discernment   D. illness

24. SUPERCILIOUS
    A. foolish   B. needless   C. callous   D. haughty

25. SPURIOUS
    A. large   B. small
    C. valid   D. not genuine

26. PREDATORY
   A. plundering   B. fawning
   C. encouraging   D. preceding

27. AMPERSAND
   A. ammunition   B. currency
   C. abbreviation   D. illumination

28. DEHYDRATED
   A. airless   B. worthless
   C. waterless   D. pointless

29. NOCTURNAL
   A. nightly   B. revolving   C. daily   D. frequently

30. DILATORY
   A. expanding B. delaying   C. watery   D. pickling

31. SANGUINE
   A. baleful   B. thirsty   C. hopeful D. delinquent

32. PHLEGMATIC
   A. sluggish   B. active   C. potent   D. secretive

33. PODIATRIST
   A. head   B. infants   C. feet   D. adults

34. INGENUE
   A. fashion   B. state   C. medicine D. stage

35. CORPOREAL
   A. military   B. naval   C. bodily   D. legal

36. MUNDANE
   A. stupid   B. ladylike   C. worldly D. weedy

37. INTERVENE
   A. induce   B. insert   C. interfere D. solve

38. IMMINENT
   A. of high renown   B. impending
   C. very large   D. incurable

39. GERMANE
   A. Teutonic   B. relevant
   C. infectious   D. brutal

40. PARITY

    A. doubt
    B. equality
    C. fitness
    D. littleness

41. RATIONALIZE

    A. rattle
    B. explain by reason
    C. limit consumption
    D. charge

42. SUCCINCT

    A. superfluous
    B. concise
    C. ponderous
    D. succulent

43. VENIAL

    A. pardonable
    B. revengeful
    C. fearful
    D. despicable

44. VERBOSITY

    A. bitterness
    B. action
    C. wordiness
    D. speed

45. WITHER

    A. canaries   B. cracks   C. decay   D. trills

46. CIRCUMVENT

    A. outwit   B. surround   C. open up   D. cover

47. COMPLICITY

    A. deceit
    B. delight in society
    C. partnership in wrong
    D. relief from debt

48. IPSO FACTO

    A. by that very fact
    B. made by hand
    C. according to him
    D. as a matter of fact

49. ABSTRUSE

    A. profound   B. absurd   C. enormous   D. ridiculous

50. RESTIVE

    A. permanent   B. quiet   C. sullen   D. impatient

KEY (CORRECT ANSWERS)

1. C	11. D	21. A	31. C	41. B
2. A	12. C	22. B	32. A	42. B
3. D	13. B	23. C	33. C	43. A
4. D	14. A	24. D	34. D	44. C
5. A	15. C	25. D	35. C	45. C
6. D	16. A	26. A	36. C	46. A
7. D	17. D	27. C	37. C	47. C
8. B	18. C	28. C	38. B	48. A
9. C	19. A	29. A	39. B	49. A
10. D	20. B	30. B	40. B	50. D

TEST 3

Questions 1-10.

DIRECTIONS: For each word listed below, one correct syllabication is shown. Indicate the CORRECT choice.

1. A. rep er cus sion   B. re per cus sion
   C. rep er cuss ion   D. re perc us sion   1.____

2. A. corr es pon dence   B. cor resp on dence
   C. cor re spond ence   D. cor res pond ence   2.____

3. A. sup er in ten dent   B. su per in ten dent
   C. su per int end ent   D. su per in tend ent   3.____

4. A. ac com mo date   B. acc om mod ate
   C. acc omm o date   D. ac com mod ate   4.____

5. A. ac know ledge   B. ac knowl edge
   C. ack nowl edge   D. ack now ledge   5.____

6. A. aud it or ium   B. au dit or ium
   C. aud i tor i um   D. au di to ri um   6.____

7. A. hosp i tal ize   B. hos pit a lize
   C. hosp it al ize   D. hos pi tal ize   7.____

8. A. du pli ca tion   B. dup lic a tion
   C. du plic a tion   D. dup li ca tion   8.____

9. A. re cap i tu late   B. rec ap it u late
   C. re ca pi tu late   D. re ca pit u late   9.____

10. A. com plim en ta ry   B. com pli men ta ry
    C. comp lim ent ar y   D. comp li ment a ry   10.____

Questions 11-25.

DIRECTIONS: In each of the following groups of sentences, there are three sentences which are correct and one which is incorrect because it contains an error in usage. Indicate the letter of the INCORRECT sentence.

11. A. There was, in the first place, no indication that a crime had been committed.   11.____
    B. She is taller than any other member of her class.
    C. She decided to leave the book lay on the table.
    D. Haven't you any film in stock at this time?

12. A. Because they had been trained for emergencies, the assault did not catch them by surprise.   12.____
    B. They divided the loot between the four of them in proportion to their effort.
    C. The number of strikes is gradually diminishing.
    D. Between acts we went out to the lobby for a brief chat.

78

13. A. It is difficult to recollect what life was like before the war. 13.____
    B. Will each of the pupils please hand their home work in?
    C. There are fewer serious mistakes in this pamphlet than I had thought.
    D. "Leave Her to Heaven" is the title of a novel by Ben Ames Williams.

14. A. I was too greatly relieved to be able to say anything. 14.____
    B. These insignia date back to ancient Roman times.
    C. We observed a strange phenomenon; the house seemed to sway in the wind and to tremble like a leaf.
    D. It would be much more preferable if you were no longer seen in his company.

15. A Please send me this data at your earliest convenience. 15.____
    A. The loss of their material proved a severe handicap.
    B. My principal objection to this plan is that it is impracticable.
    C. The doll has lain in the rain all evening.

16. A. I had expected to see my brother. 16.____
    B. He expected to have seen his brother.
    C. I hoped to see you do better.
    D. It was his duty to assist our friend.

17. A. The reason why I am writing to you is that I wish to avoid further misunderstanding. 17.____
    B. These kind of arguments always cause hard feelings.
    C. Regardless of your decision, I shall have to go.
    D. I have only twenty pupils in this class.

18. A. Which is the youngest of the two sisters? 18.____
    B. I am determined to finish the work before Saturday.
    C. It is difficult to see why the problems are not correctly solved.
    D. I have never met a more interesting person.

19. A. Located on a mountainside with a babbling brook beside the door, it was a dream palace. 19.____
    B. Blessed are they that have not seen and yet have believed.
    C. The customs in that part of the country are much different than I expected.
    D. Politics, even in towns of small population, has always attracted ambitious young lawyers.

20. A. Of all my friends he is the one on whom I can most surely depend. 20.____
    B. We value the Constitution because of it's guarantees to freedom.
    C. The audience was deeply stirred by the actor's performance .
    D. Give the book to whoever comes into the room first.

21. A. Everything was in order: the paper ruled, the pencils sharpened, the chairs placed. 21.____
    B. Neither John nor Peter were able to attend the reception.
    C. In April the streets which had been damaged by cold weather were repaired by the workmen.
    D. You may lend my book to the pupil who you think will enjoy it most.

22. A. He fidgeted, like most children do, while the grown-ups were discussing the problem.
    B. I won't go unless you go with me.
    C. Sitting beside the charred ruins of his cabin, the frontiersman told us the story of the attack.
    D. Certainly there can be no objection to the boys" working on a volunteer basis.

    22.____

23. A. The congregation was dismissed.
    B. The congregation were deeply moved by the sermon.
    C. What kind of an automobile is that?
    D. His explanation and mine agree.

    23.____

24. A. There is no danger of him being elected.
    B. There is no doubt of his election.
    C. John and he are to be the speakers.
    D. John and she are to be the speakers.

    24.____

25. A. Them that honor me I will honor.
    B. They that believe in me shall be rewarded.
    C. Who did you see at the meeting?
    D. Whom are you writing to?

    25.____

KEY (CORRECT ANSWERS)

1. B
2. C
3. D
4. A
5. B

6. D
7. D
8. A
9. D
10. B

11. C
12. B
13. B
14. D
15. A

16. B
17. B
18. A
19. C
20. B

21. B
22. A
23. C
24. A
25. C

EXAMINATION SECTION
TEST 1

DIRECTIONS: Each question or incomplete statement is followed by several suggested answers or completions. Select the one that BEST answers the question or completes the statement. *PRINT THE LETTER OF THE CORRECT ANSWER IN THE SPACE AT THE RIGHT.*

Questions 1-22.

DIRECTIONS: Read through each group of words. Indicate in the space at the right the letter of the misspelled word.

1. A. miniature B. recession C. accommodate D. supress 1.____

2. A. mortgage B. illogical C. fasinate D. pronounce 2.____

3. A. calendar B. heros C. ecstasy D. librarian 3.____

4. A. initiative B. extraordinary C. villian D. exaggerate 4.____

5. A. absence B. sense C. dosn't D. height 5.____

6. A. curiosity B. ninety C. truely D. grammar 6.____

7. A. amateur B. definate C. meant D. changeable 7.____

8. A. excellent B. studioes C. achievement D. weird 8.____

9. A. goverment B. description C. sergeant D. desirable 9.____

10. A. proceed B. anxious C. neice D. precede 10.____

11. A. environment B. omitted C. apparant D. misconstrue 11.____

12. A. comparative B. hindrance C. benefited D. unamimous 12.____

13. A. embarrass   B. recommend   13.____
    C. desciple   D. argument

14. A. sophomore   B. suprintendent   14.____
    C. concievable D. disastrous

15. A. agressive   B. questionnaire   15.____
    C. occurred   D. rhythm

16. A. peaceable   B. conscientious   16.____
    C. redicule   D. deterrent

17. A. mischievious B. writing   17.____
    C. competition D. athletics

18. A. auxiliary   B. synonymous   18.____
    C. maneuver   D. repitition

19. A. existence   B. optomistic   19.____
    C. acquitted   D. tragedy

20. A. hypocrisy   B. parrallel   20.____
    C. exhilaration D. prevalent

21. A. convalesence B. infallible   21.____
    C. destitute   D. grotesque

22. A. magnanimity B. asassination   22.____
    C. incorrigible D. pestilence

Questions 23-40.

DIRECTIONS: In Questions 23 through 40, one sentence fragment contains an error in punctuation or capitalization. Indicate the letter of the INCORRECT sentence fragment and place it in the space at the right.

23. A. Despite a year's work   23.____
    B. in a well-equipped laboratory
    C. my Uncle failed to complete his research
    D. now he will never graduate.

24. A. Gene, if you are going to sleep   24.____
    B. all afternoon I will enter
    C. that ladies' golf tournament
    D. sponsored by the Chamber of Commerce.

25. A. Seeing the cat slink toward the barn,
    B. the farmer's wife jumped off the
    C. ladder picked up a broom, and began
    D. shouting at the top of her voice.

    25.____

26. A. Extending over southeast Idaho and
    B. northwest Wyoming, the Tetons
    C. are noted for their height; however the
    D. highest peak is actually under 14,000 feet.

    26.____

27. A. "Sarah, can you recall the name
    B. of the English queen
    C. who supposedly said, 'We are not
    D. amused?"

    27.____

28. A. My aunt's graduation present to me
    B. cost, I imagine more than she could
    C. actually afford. It's a
    D. Swiss watch with numerous features.

    28.____

29. A. On the left are examples of buildings
    B. from the Classical Period; two temples
    C. one of which was dedicated to Zeus; the
    D. Agora, a marketplace; and a large arch.

    29.____

30. A. Tired of sonic booms, the people who
    B. live near Springfield's Municipal Airport
    C. formed an anti noise organization
    D. with the amusing name of Sound Off.

    30.____

31. A. "Joe, Mrs. Sweeney said, "your family
    B. arrives Sunday. Since you'll be in
    C. the Labor Day parade, we could ask Mr.
    D. Krohn, who has a big car, to meet them."

    31.____

32. A. The plumber emerged from the basement and
    B. said, "Mr. Cohen I found the trouble in
    C. your water heater. Could you move those
    D. Schwinn bikes out of my way?"

    32.____

33. A. The President walked slowly to the
    B. podium, bowed to Edward Everett Hale
    C. the other speaker, and began his formal address:
    D. "Fourscore and seven years ago...."

    33.____

34. A. Mr. Fontana, I hope, will arrive before
    B. the beginning of the ceremonies; however,
    C. if his plane is delayed, I have a substitute
    D. speaker who can be here at a moments' notice.

    34.____

35. A. Gladys wedding dress, a satin creation,
    B. lay crumpled on the floor; her veil,
    C. torn and streaked, lay nearby. "Jilted!"
    D. shrieked Gladys. She was clearly annoyed.

    35.____

36. A. Although it is poor grammar, the word
    B. hopefully has become television's newest
    C. pet expression; I hope (to use the correct
    D. form) that it will soon pass from favor.

    36.____

37. A.   Plaza Apartment Hotel
    B.   103 Tower road
    C.   Hampstead, Iowa 52025
    D.   March 13, 2021

    37.____

38. A. Circulation Department
    B. British History Illustrated
    C. 3000 Walnut Street
    D. Boulder Colorado 80302

    38.____

39. A. Dear Sirs:
    B. Last spring I ordered a subscription to your
    C. magazine. I had read and enjoyed the May
    D. issue containing the article titled "kings."

    39.____

40. A. I have not however, received a
    B. single issue. Will you check this?
    C. Sincerely,
    D. Maria Herrera

    40.____

Questions 41-70.

DIRECTIONS: Questions 41 through 70 represent common grammatical concerns: subject-verb agreement, appropriate use of pronouns, and appropriate use of verbs. Read each sentence and indicate the letter of the grammatically CORRECT answer in the space at the right.

41. THE REIVERS, one of William Faulkner's last works, _____ made into a movie starring Steve McQueen.
    A. has been   B. have been   C. are being   D. were

    41.____

42. He _____ on the ground, his eyes fastened on an ant slowly pushing a morsel of food toward the ant hill.
    A. layed   B. laid   C. had laid   D. lay

    42.____

43. Nobody in the tri-cities _____ to admit that a flood could be disastrous.
    A. are willing   B. have been willing
    C. is willing   D. were willing

    43.____

44. "_____," the senator asked, "have you convinced to run against the incumbent?"
    A. Who   B. Whom   C. Whomever   D. Womsoever

45. Of all the psychology courses that I took, Statistics 101 _____ the most demanding.
    A. was   B. are   C. is   D. were

46. Neither the conductor nor the orchestra members _____ the music to be applauded so enthusiastically.
    A. were expecting
    B. was expecting
    C. is expected
    D. has been expecting

47. The requirements for admission to the Lettermen's Club _____ posted outside the athletic director's office for months.
    A. was   B. was being   C. has been   D. have been

48. Please give me a list of the people _____ to compete in the kayak race.
    A. whom you think have planned
    B. who you think has planned
    C. who you think is planning
    D. who you think are planning

49. I saw Eloise and Abelard earlier today; _____ were riding around in a fancy 1956 MG.
    A. she and him   B. her and him   C. she and he   D. her and he

50. If you _____ the trunk in the attic, I'll unpack it later today.
    A. can sit
    B. are able to sit
    C. can set
    D. have sat

51. _____ all of the flour been used, or may I borrow three cups?
    A. Have   B. Has   C. Is   D. Could

52. In exasperation, the cycle shop's owner suggested that _____ there too long.
    A. us boys were
    B. we boys were
    C. us boys had been
    D. we boys had been

53. Idleness as well as money _____ the root of all evil.
    A. have been
    B. were to have been
    C. is
    D. are

54. Only the string players from the quartet—Gregory, Isaac, _____—remained after the concert to answer questions.
    A. him, and I
    B. he, and I
    C. him, and me
    D. he, and me

55. Of all the antiques that _____ for sale, Gertrude chose to buy a stupid glass thimble.
    A. was
    B. is
    C. would have
    D. were

56. The detective snapped, "Don't confuse me with theories about _____ you believe committed the crime!"
    A. who   B. whom   C. whomever   D. which

57. _____ when we first called, we might have avoided our present predicament.
    A. The plumber's coming
    B. If the plumber would have come
    C. If the plumber had come
    D. If the plumber was to have come

58. We thought the sun _____ in the north until we discovered that our compass was defective.
    A. had rose
    B. had risen
    C. had rised
    D. had raised

59. Each play of Shakespeare's _____ more than _____ share of memorable characters.
    A. contain its
    B. contains; its
    C. contains; it's
    D. contain; their

60. Our English teacher suggested to _____ seniors that either Tolstoy or Dickens _____ the outstanding novelist of the nineteenth century.
    A. we; was considered
    B. we; were considered
    C. us; was considered
    D. us; were considered

61. Sherlock Holmes, together with his great friend and companion Dr. Watson, _____ to aid the woman _____ had stumbled into the room.
    A. has agreed; who
    B. have agreed; whom
    C. has agreed; whom
    D. have agreed; who

62. Several of the deer _____ when they spotted my backpack _____ open in the meadow.
    A. was frightened; laying
    B. were frightened; lying
    C. were frightened; laying
    D. was frightened; lying

63. After the Scholarship Committee announces _____ selection, hysterics often _____.
    A. it's; occur
    B. its; occur
    C. their; occur
    D. their; occurs

64. I _____ the key on the table last night so you and _____ could find it.
    A. layed; her
    B. lay; she
    C. laid; she
    D. laid; her

65. Some of the antelope _____ wandered away from the meadow where the rancher _____ the block of salt.
    A. has; sat
    B. has; set
    C. have; had set
    D. has; sets

66. Macaroni and cheese _____ best to us (that is, to Andy and _____) when Mother adds extra cheddar cheese.
    A. tastes; I
    B. tastes; me
    C. taste; me
    D. taste; I

66._____

67. Frank said, "It must have been _____ called the phone company."
    A. she who
    B. she whom
    C. her who
    D. her whom

67._____

68. The herd _____ moving restlessly at every bolt of lightning; it was either Ted or _____ who saw the beginning of the stampede.
    A. was; me
    B. were; I
    C. was; I
    D. have been; me

68._____

69. The foreman _____ his lateness by saying that his alarm clock _____ until six minutes before eight.
    A. explains; had not rang
    B. explained; has not rung
    C. has explained; rung
    D. explained; hadn't rung

69._____

70. Of all the coaches, Ms. Cox is the only one who _____ that Sherry dives more gracefully than _____.
    A. is always saying; I
    B. is always saying; me
    C. are always saying; I
    D. were always saying; me

70._____

Questions 71-90.

DIRECTIONS: Choose the word in Questions 71 through 90 that is MOST opposite in meaning to the italicized word.

71. *fact*
    A. statistic
    B. statement
    C. incredible
    D. conjecture

71._____

72. *stiff*
    A. fastidious
    B. babble
    C. supple
    D. apprehensive

72._____

73. *blunt*
    A. concise   B. tactful   C. artistic   D. humble

73._____

74. *foreign*
    A. pertinent   B. comely   C. strange   D. scrupulous

74._____

75. *anger*
    A. infer   B. pacify   C. taint   D. revile

75._____

76. *frank*
    A. earnest   B. reticent   C. post   D. expensive

76._____

77. *secure*
    A. precarious   B. acquire   C. moderate   D. frenzied

78. *petty*
    A. harmonious   B. careful
    C. forthright   D. momentous

79. *concede*
    A. dispute   B. reciprocate
    C. subvert   D. propagate

80. *benefit*
    A. liquidation   B. bazaar
    C. detriment   D. profit

81. *capricious*
    A. preposterous   B. constant
    C. diabolical   D. careless

82. *boisterous*
    A. devious   B. valiant   C. girlish   D. taciturn

83. *harmony*
    A. congruence   B. discord   C. chagrin   D. melody

84. *laudable*
    A. auspicious   B. despicable
    C. acclaimed   D. doubtful

85. *adherent*
    A. partisan   B. stoic   C. renegade   D. recluse

86. *exuberant*
    A. frail   B. corpulent   C. austere   D. bigot

87. *spurn*
    A. accede   B. flail   C. efface   D. annihilate

88. *spontaneous*
    A. hapless   B. corrosive
    C. intentional   D. willful

89. *disparage*
    A. abolish   B. exude   C. incriminate   D. extol

90. *timorous*
    A. succinct   B. chaste   C. audacious   D. insouciant

KEY (CORRECT ANSWERS)

1. D	21. A	41. A	61. A	81. B
2. C	22. B	42. D	62.	82. D
3. B	23. C	43. C	63. B	83. B
4. C	24. B	44. B	64. C	84. B
5. C	25. C	45. A	65. C	85. C
6. C	26. C	46. A	66. B	86. C
7. B	27. D	47. D	67. A	87. A
8. B	28. B	48. A	68. C	88. C
9. A	29. B	49. C	69. D	89. D
10. C	30. C	50. C	70. A	90. C
11. C	31. A	51. B	71. D	
12. D	32. B	52. D	72. C	
13. C	33. B	53. C	73. B	
14. C	34. D	54. B	74. A	
15. A	35. A	55. D	75. B	
16. C	36. B	56. B	76. B	
17. A	37. B	57. C	77. A	
18. D	38. D	58. B	78. D	
19. B	39. D	59. B	79. A	
20. B	40. A	60. C	80. C	

EXAMINATION SECTION
TEST 1

DIRECTIONS: In each of the following tests in this part, select the letter of the one MIS-SPELLED word in each of the following groups of words. If no word is misspelled, select the last item, letter E (none misspelled). *PRINT THE LETTER OF THE CORRECT ANSWER IN THE SPACE AT THE RIGHT.*

1. A. grateful B. fundimental C. census 1.____
   D. analysis E. NONE MISSPELLED

2. A. installment B. retrieve C. concede 2.____
   D. dissapear E. NONE MISSPELLED

3. A. accidentaly B. dismissal C. conscientious 3.____
   D. indelible E. NONE MISSPELLED

4. A. perceive B. carreer C. anticipate 4.____
   D. acquire E. NONE MISSPELLED

5. A. facility B. reimburse C. assortment 5.____
   D. guidance E. NONE MISSPELLED

6. A. plentiful B. across C. advantagous 6.____
   D. similar E. NONE MISSPELLED

7. A. omission B. pamphlet C. guarrantee 7.____
   D. repel E. NONE MISSPELLED

8. A. maintenance B. always C. liable 8.____
   D. anouncement E. NONE MISSPELLED

9. A. exaggerate B. sieze C. condemn 9.____
   D. commit E. NONE MISSPELLED

10. A. pospone B. altogether C. grievance 10.____
    D. excessive E. NONE MISSPELLED

11. A. arguing B. correspondance C. forfeit 11.____
    D. dissension E. NONE MISSPELLED

12. A. occasion B. description C. prejudice 12.____
    D. elegible E. NONE MISSPELLED

13. A. accomodate B. initiative C. changeable 13.____
    D. enroll E. NONE MISSPELLED

14. A. temporary B. insistent C. benificial 14.____
    D. separate E. NONE MISSPELLED

15. A. achieve B. dissapoint C. unanimous 15.____
    D. judgment E. NONE MISSPELLED

16. A. proceed B. publicly C. sincerity 16.____
    D. successful E. NONE MISSPELLED

17.	A. deceive D. repetitive		B. goverment E. *NONE MISSPELLED*		C. preferable	17.___
18.	A. emphasis D. optimistic		B. skillful E. *NONE MISSPELLED*		C. advisible	18.___
19.	A. tendency D. noticable		B. rescind E. *NONE MISSPELLED*		C. crucial	19.___
20.	A. privelege D. divisible		B. abbreviate E. *NONE MISSPELLED*		C. simplify	20.___

KEY (CORRECT ANSWERS)

1. B. fundamental
2. D. disappear
3. A. accidentally
4. B. career
5. E. None Misspelled
6. C. advantageous
7. C. guarantee
8. D. announcement
9. B. seize
10. A. postpone
11. B. correspondence
12. D. eligible
13. A. accommodate
14. C. beneficial
15. B. disappoint
16. E. None Misspelled
17. B. government
18. C. advisable
19. D. noticeable
20. A. privilege

TEST 2

DIRECTIONS: In each of the following tests in this part, select the letter of the one MISSPELLED word in each of the following groups of words. If no word is misspelled, select the last item, letter E (none misspelled). *PRINT THE LETTER OF THE CORRECT ANSWER IN THE SPACE AT THE RIGHT.*

1. A. typical B. descend C. summarize 1._____
   D. continuel E. NONE MISSPELLED

2. A. courageous B. recomend C. omission 2._____
   D. eliminate E. NONE MISSPELLED

3. A. compliment B. illuminate C. auxilary 3._____
   D. installation E. NONE MISSPELLED

4. A. preliminary B. aquainted C. syllable 4._____
   D. analysis E. NONE MISSPELLED

5. A. accustomed B. negligible C. interupted 5._____
   D. bulletin E. NONE MISSPELLED

6. A. summoned B. managment C. mechanism 6._____
   D. sequence E. NONE MISSPELLED

7. A. commitee B. surprise C. noticeable 7._____
   D. emphasize E. NONE MISSPELLED

8. A. occurrance B. likely C. accumulate 8._____
   D. grievance E. grievance

9. A. obstacle B. particuliar C. baggage 9._____
   D. fascinating E. NONE MISSPELLED

10. A. innumerable B. seize C. applicant 10._____
    D. dicionery E. NONE MISSPELLED

11. A. primary B. mechanic C. referred 11._____
    D. admissible E. NONE MISSPELLED

12. A. cessation B. beleif C. aggressive 12._____
    D. allowance E. NONE MISSPELLED

13. A. leisure B. authentic C. familiar 13._____
    D. contemptable E. NONE MISSPELLED

14. A. volume B. forty C. dilemma 14._____
    D. seldum E. NONE MISSPELLED

15. A. discrepancy B. aquisition C. exorbitant 15._____
    D. lenient E. NONE MISSPELLED

16. A. simultanous B. penetrate C. revision 16._____
    D. conspicuous E. NONE MISSPELLED

17. A. ilegible B. gracious C. profitable 17._____
    D. obedience E. NONE MISSPELLED

18. A. manufacturer   B. authorize   C. compelling   18.____
    D. pecular   E. *NONE MISSPELLED*

19. A. anxious   B. rehearsal   C. handicaped   19.____
    D. tendency   E. *NONE MISSPELLED*

20. A. meticulous   B. accompaning   C. initiative   20.____
    D. shelves   E. *NONE MISSPELLED*

KEY (CORRECT ANSWERS)

1. D. continual
2. B. recommend
3. C. auxiliary
4. B. acquainted
5. C. interrupted
6. B. management
7. A. committee
8. A. occurrence
9. B. particular
10. D. dictionary
11. E. None Misspelled
12. B. belief
13. D. contemptible
14. D. seldom
15. B. acquisition
16. A. simultaneous
17. A. illegible
18. D. peculiar
19. C. handicapped
20. B. accompanying

TEST 3

DIRECTIONS: In each of the following tests in this part, select the letter of the one MISSPELLED word in each of the following groups of words. If no word is misspelled, select the last item, letter E (none misspelled). *PRINT THE LETTER OF THE CORRECT ANSWER IN THE SPACE AT THE RIGHT.*

1. A. grievous B. dilettante C. gibberish 1.____
   D. upbraid E. *NONE MISSPELLED*

2. A. embarrassing B. playright C. unmanageable 2.____
   D. symmetrical E. *NONE MISSPELLED*

3. A. sestet B. denouement C. liaison 3.____
   D. tattooing E. *NONE MISSPELLED*

4. A. prophesied B. soliliquy C. supersede 4.____
   D. hemorrhage E. *NONE MISSPELLED*

5. A. colossal B. renascent C. parallel 5.____
   D. omnivorous E. *NONE MISSPELLED*

6. A. passable B. dispensable C. deductable 6.____
   D. irreducible E. *NONE MISSPELLED*

7. A. guerrila B. carousal C. maneuver 7.____
   D. staid E. *NONE MISSPELLED*

8. A. maintenance B. mountainous C. sustenance 8.____
   D. gluttinous E. *NONE MISSPELLED*

9. A. holocaust B. irascible C. buccanneer 9.____
   D. mischievous E. *NONE MISSPELLED*

10. A. diphthong B. rhododendron C. inviegle 10.____
    D. shellacked E. *NONE MISSPELLED*

11. A. Phillipines B. currant C. dietitian 11.____
    D. coercion E. *NONE MISSPELLED*

12. A. courtesey B. buoyancy C. fiery 12.____
    D. shepherd E. *NONE MISSPELLED*

13. A. censor B. queue C. obbligato 13.____
    D. antartic E. *NONE MISSPELLED*

14. A. chrystal B. chrysanthemum C. chrysalis 14.____
    D. chrome E. *NONE MISSPELLED*

15. A. shreik B. siege C. sheik 15.____
    D. sieve E. *NONE MISSPELLED*

16. A. leisure B. gladioluses C. kindergarden 16.____
    D. tonnage E. *NONE MISSPELLED*

17. A. emminent B. imminent C. blatant 17.____
    D. privilege E. *NONE MISSPELLED*

95

18. A. diphtheria   B. collander   C. seize   18.____
    D. sleight   E. *NONE MISSPELLED*

19. A. frolicking   B. caramel   C. germaine   19.____
    D. kohlrabi   E. *NONE MISSPELLED*

20. A. dispensable B. compatable C. recommend 20.____
    D. feasible   E. *NONE MISSPELLED*

KEY (CORRECT ANSWERS)

1. E. None Misspelled
2. B. playwright
3. E. None Misspelled
4. B. soliloquy
5. E. None Misspelled
6. C. deductible
7. A. guerrilla
8. D. gluttonous
9. C. buccaneer
10. C. inveigle
11. A. Philippines
12. A. courtesy
13. D. antarctic
14. A. crystal
15. A. shriek
16. C. kindergarten
17. A. eminent
18. B. colander
19. C. germane
20. B. compatible

TEST 4

DIRECTIONS: In each of the following tests in this part, select the letter of the one MISSPELLED word in each of the following groups of words. If no word is misspelled, select the last item, letter E (none misspelled). *PRINT THE LETTER OF THE CORRECT ANSWER IN THE SPACE AT THE RIGHT.*

1. A. coercion B. rescission C. license 1.____
   D. prophecied E. *NONE MISSPELLED*

2. A. calcimine B. seive C. procedure 2.____
   D. poinsettia E. *NONE MISSPELLED*

3. A. entymology B. echoing C. subtly 3.____
   D. stupefy E. *NONE MISSPELLED*

4. A. mocassin B. assassin C. battalion 4.____
   D. despicable E. *NONE MISSPELLED*

5. A. moustache B. sovereignty C. drunkeness 5.____
   D. staccato E. *NONE MISSPELLED*

6. A. notoriety B. stereotype C. trellis 6.____
   D. Uraguay E. *NONE MISSPELLED*

7. A. hummock B. idiosyncrasy C. licentiate 7.____
   D. plagiarism E. *NONE MISSPELLED*

8. A. denim B. hyssop C. innoculate 8.____
   D. malevolent E. *NONE MISSPELLED*

9. A. boundaries B. corpulency C. gauge 9.____
   D. jingoes E. *NONE MISSPELLED*

10. A. assassin B. refulgeant C. sorghum 10.____
    D. suture E. *NONE MISSPELLED*

11. A. dormatory B. glimpse C. mediocre 11.____
    D. repetition E. *NONE MISSPELLED*

12. A. ambergris B. docility C. loquacious 12.____
    D. Pharoah E. *NONE MISSPELLED*

13. A. curriculum B. ninety-eighth C. occurrence 13.____
    D. repertoire E. *NONE MISSPELLED*

14. A. belladonna B. equable C. immersion 14.____
    D. naphtha E. *NONE MISSPELLED*

15. A. itinerary B. ptomaine C. similar 15.____
    D. solicetous E. *NONE MISSPELLED*

16. A. liquify B. mausoleum C. Philippines 16.____
    D. singeing E. *NONE MISSPELLED*

17. A. descendant B. harrassed C. implausible 17.____
    D. irreverence E. *NONE MISSPELLED*

18. A. crystallize   B. imperceptible   C. isinglass   18.___
    D. precede   E. *NONE MISSPELLED*

19. A. accommodate B. deferential   C. gazeteer   19.___
    D. plenteous   E. *NONE MISSPELLED*

20. A. aching   B. buttress   C. indigenous 20.___
    D. mischievous   E. *NONE MISSPELLED*

KEY (CORRECT ANSWERS)

1. D. prophesied
2. B. sieve
3. A. entomology
4. A. moccasin
5. C. drunkenness
6. D. Uruguay
7. E. None Misspelled
8. C. inoculate
9. E. None Misspelled
10. B. refulgent
11. A. dormitory
12. D. Pharaoh
13. E. None Misspelled
14. E. None misspelled
15. D. solicitous
16. A. liquefy
17. B. harassed
18. E. None Misspelled
19. C. gazetteer
20. E. None Misspelled

TEST 5

DIRECTIONS: In each of the following tests in this part, select the letter of the one MISSPELLED word in each of the following groups of words. If no word is misspelled, select the last item, letter E (none misspelled). *PRINT THE LETTER OF THE CORRECT ANSWER IN THE SPACE AT THE RIGHT.*

1. A. comensurable B. fracas C. obeisance 1.____
   D. remittent E. *NONE MISSPELLED*

2. A. defiance B. delapidated C. motley 2.____
   D. rueful E. *NONE MISSPELLED*

3. A. demeanor B. epoch C. furtive 3.____
   D. parley E. *NONE MISSPELLED*

4. A. disciples B. influencial C. nemesis 4.____
   D. poultry E. *NONE MISSPELLED*

5. A. decision B. encourage C. incidental 5.____
   D. satyr E. *NONE MISSPELLED*

6. A. collate B. connivance C. luxurient 6.____
   D. manageable E. *NONE MISSPELLED*

7. A. constituencies B. crocheted C. foreclosure 7.____
   D. scintillating E. *NONE MISSPELLED*

8. A. arraignment B. assassination C. carburator 8.____
   D. irrationally E. *NONE MISSPELLED*

9. A. livelihood B. noticeable C. optomiatic 9.____
   D. psychology E. *NONE MISSPELLED*

10. A. daub B. massacre C. repitition 10.____
    D. requiem E. *NONE MISSPELLED*

11. A. adversary B. beneficiary C. cemetery 11.____
    D. desultory E. *NONE MISSPELLED*

12. A. criterion B. elicit C. incredulity 12.____
    D. omnishient E. *NONE MISSPELLED*

13. A. dining B. fiery C. incidentally 13.____
    D. rheumatism E. *NONE MISSPELLED*

14. A. collaborator B. gaudey C. habilitation 14.____
    D. logician E. *NONE MISSPELLED*

15. A. dirge B. ogle C. recumbent 15.____
    D. reminiscence E. *NONE MISSPELLED*

16. A. conscientious B. renunciation C. inconvenient 16.____
    D. inoculate E. *NONE MISSPELLED*

17. A. crystalline B. scimitar C. ecstacy 17.____
    D. vestigial E. *NONE MISSPELLED*

99

18. A. phlegmatic   B. rhythm   C. plebescite   18.___
    D. refectory   E. *NONE MISSPELLED*

19. A. resilient   B. resevoir   C. recipient   19.___
    D. sobriety   E. *NONE MISSPELLED*

20. A. privilege   B. leige   C. leisure   20.___
    D. basilisk   E. *NONE MISSPELLED*

KEY (CORRECT ANSWERS)

1. A. commensurable
2. B. dilapidated
3. E. None Misspelled
4. B. influential
5. E. None Misspelled
6. C. luxuriant
7. E. None Misspelled
8. C. carburetor
9. C. optimistic
10. C. repetition
11. E. None Misspelled
12. D. omniscient
13. E. None Misspelled
14. B. gaudy
15. E. None Misspelled
16. E. None Misspelled
17. C. ecstasy
18. C. plebiscite
19. B. reservoir
20. B. liege

TEST 6

DIRECTIONS: In each of the following tests in this part, select the letter of the one MISSPELLED word in each of the following groups of words. If no word is misspelled, select the last item, letter E (none misspelled). *PRINT THE LETTER OF THE CORRECT ANSWER IN THE SPACE AT THE RIGHT.*

1. A. repellent B. elliptical C. paralelling 1.____
   D. colossal E. NONE MISSPELLED

2. A. uproarious B. grievous C. armature 2.____
   D. tabular E. NONE MISSPELLED

3. A. ammassed B. embarrassed C. promissory 3.____
   D. asymmetrical E. NONE MISSPELLED

4. A. maintenance B. correspondence C. benificence 4.____
   D. miasmic E. NONE MISSPELLED

5. A. demurred B. occurrence C. temperament 5.____
   D. abhorrance E. NONE MISSPELLED

6. A. proboscis B. lucious C. mischievous 6.____
   D. vilify E. NONE MISSPELLED

7. A. feasable B. divisible C. permeable 7.____
   D. forcible E. NONE MISSPELLED

8. A. courteous B. venemous C. heterogeneous 8.____
   D. lustrous E. NONE MISSPELLED

9. A. millionaire B. mayonnaise C. questionaire 9.____
   D. silhouette E. NONE MISSPELLED

10. A. contemptible B. irreverent C. illimitable 10.____
    D. inveigled E. NONE MISSPELLED

11. A. prevalent B. irrelavent C. ecstasy 11.____
    D. auxiliary E. NONE MISSPELLED

12. A. impeccable B. raillery C. precede 12.____
    D. occurrence E. NONE MISSPELLED

13. A. patrolling B. vignette C. ninety 13.____
    D. surveilance E. NONE MISSPELLED

14. A. holocaust B. incidently C. weird 14.____
    D. canceled E. NONE MISSPELLED

15. A. emmendation B. gratuitous C. fissionable 15.____
    D. dilemma E. NONE MISSPELLED

16. A. harass B. innuendo C. capilary 16.____
    D. pachyderm E. NONE MISSPELLED

17. A. concomitant B. Lilliputian C. sarcophagus 17.____
    D. melifluous E. NONE MISSPELLED

101

18. A. interpolate B. disident C. venal 18.____
    D. inveigh E. *NONE MISSPELLED*

19. A. supercillious B. biennial C. gargantuan 19.____
    D. irresistible E. *NONE MISSPELLED*

20. A. conniving B. expedite C. inflammible 20.____
    D. incorruptible E. *NONE MISSPELLED*

KEY (CORRECT ANSWERS)

1. C. paralleling
2. E. None Misspelled
3. A. amassed
4. C. beneficence
5. D. abhorrence
6. B. luscious
7. A. feasible
8. B. venomous
9. C. questionnaire
10. E. None Misspelled
11. B. irrelevant
12. E. None Misspelled
13. D. surveillance
14. B. incidentally
15. A. emendation
16. C. capillary
17. D. mellifluous
18. B. dissident
19. A. supercilious
20. C. inflammable

TEST 7

DIRECTIONS: In each of the following tests in this part, select the letter of the one MISSPELLED word in each of the following groups of words. If no word is misspelled, select the last item, letter E (none misspelled). *PRINT THE LETTER OF THE CORRECT ANSWER IN THE SPACE AT THE RIGHT.*

1. A. torturous B. omniscient C. hymenial 1.____
   D. flaccid E. *NONE MISSPELLED*

2. A. seige B. seize C. frieze 2.____
   D. grieve E. *NONE MISSPELLED*

3. A. indispensible B. euphony C. victuals 3.____
   D. receptacle E. *NONE MISSPELLED*

4. A. schism B. fortissimo C. innocuous 4.____
   D. epicurian E. *NONE MISSPELLED*

5. A. sustenance B. vilefy C. maintenance 5.____
   D. rarefy E. *NONE MISSPELLED*

6. A. desiccated B. alleviate C. beneficence 6.____
   D. preponderance E. *NONE MISSPELLED*

7. A. battalion B. incubus C. sacrilegious 7.____
   D. innert E. *NONE MISSPELLED*

8. A. shiboleth B. connoisseur C. potpourri 8.____
   D. dichotomy E. *NONE MISSPELLED*

9. A. pamphlet B. similar C. parlament 9.____
   D. benefited E. *NONE MISSPELLED*

10. A. genealogy B. tyrannical C. diletante 10.____
    D. abhorrence E. *NONE MISSPELLED*

11. A. effeminate B. concensus C. agglomeration 11.____
    D. fission E. *NONE MISSPELLED*

12. A. narcissus B. lyceum C. odissey 12.____
    D. peccadillo E. *NONE MISSPELLED*

13. A. stupefied B. psychiatry C. onerous 13.____
    D. frieze E. *NONE MISSPELLED*

14. A. intelligible B. semaphore C. pronounciation 14.____
    D. albumen E. *NONE MISSPELLED*

15. A. annihilate B. tyrannical C. occurence 15.____
    D. allergy E. *NONE MISSPELLED*

16. A. gauging B. probossis C. specimen 16.____
    D. its E. *NONE MISSPELLED*

17. A. diphthong B. connoisseur C. iresistible 17.____
    D. dilemma E. *NONE MISSPELLED*

18. A. affect B. baccillus C. beige
    D. seize E. *NONE MISSPELLED*

19. A. apostasy B. sustenance C. synonym
    D. epigrammatic E. *NONE MISSPELLED*

20. A. discernable B. consul C. efflorescence
    D. complement E. *NONE MISSPELLED*

KEY (CORRECT ANSWERS)

1. C. hymeneal
2. A. siege
3. A. indispensable
4. D. epicurean
5. B. vilify
6. E. None Misspelled
7. D. inert
8. A. shibboleth
9. C. parliament
10. C. dilettante
11. B. consensus
12. C. odyssey
13. E. None Misspelled
14. C. pronunciation
15. C. occurrence
16. B. proboscis
17. C. irresistible
18. B. bacillus
19. E. None Misspelled
20. A. discernible

TEST 8

DIRECTIONS: In each of the following tests in this part, select the letter of the one MIS-SPELLED word in each of the following groups of words. If no word is misspelled, select the last item, letter E (none misspelled). *PRINT THE LETTER OF THE CORRECT ANSWER IN THE SPACE AT THE RIGHT.*

1. A. righteous B. seafareing C. colloquial 1.____
   D. contumely E. *NONE MISSPELLED*

2. A. sanitarium B. vicissitude C. mischievious 2.____
   D. chlorophyll E. *NONE MISSPELLED*

3. A. captain B. theirs C. asceticism 3.____
   D. acquiesced E. *NONE MISSPELLED*

4. A. across B. her's C. democracy 4.____
   D. signature E. *NONE MISSPELLED*

5. A. villain B. vacillate C. imposter 5.____
   D. temperament E. *NONE MISSPELLED*

6. A. idyllic B. volitile C. obloquy 6.____
   D. emendation E. *NONE MISSPELLED*

7. A. heinous B. sattelite C. dissident 7.____
   D. ephemeral E. *NONE MISSPELLED*

8. A. ennoble B. shellacked C. vilify 8.____
   D. indissoluble E. *NONE MISSPELLED*

9. A. argueing B. intrepid C. papyrus 9.____
   D. foulard E. *NONE MISSPELLED*

10. A. guttural B. acknowleging C. isosceles 10.____
    D. assonance E. *NONE MISSPELLED*

11. A. shoeing B. exorcise C. development 11.____
    D. irreperable E. *NONE MISSPELLED*

12. A. counseling B. cancellation C. kidnapped 12.____
    D. repellant E. *NONE MISSPELLED*

13. A. disatisfy B. misstep C. usually 13.____
    D. gregarious E. *NONE MISSPELLED*

14. A. unparalleled B. beggar C. embarrass 14.____
    D. ecstacy E. *NONE MISSPELLED*

15. A. descendant B. poliomyelitis C. privilege 15.____
    D. tragedy E. *NONE MISSPELLED*

16. A. nullify B. siderial C. salability 16.____
    D. irrelevant E. *NONE MISSPELLED*

17. A. paraphenalia B. apothecaries C. occurrence 17.____
    D. plagiarize E. *NONE MISSPELLED*

18.	A. asinine D. indispensable	B. dissonent E. *NONE MISSPELLED*	C. opossum	18.___
19.	A. orifice D. accommodate	B. deferrment E. *NONE MISSPELLED*	C. harass	19.___
20.	A. changeable D. dissatisfy	B. therefor E. *NONE MISSPELLED*	C. incidently	20.___

KEY (CORRECT ANSWERS)

1. B. seafaring
2. C. mischievous
3. E. None Misspelled
4. B. hers
5. C. impostor
6. B. volatile
7. B. satellite
8. E. None Misspelled
9. A. arguing
10. B. acknowledging
11. D. irreparable
12. D. repellent
13. A. dissatisfy
14. D. ecstasy
15. E. None Misspelled
16. B. sidereal
17. A. paraphernalia
18. B. dissonant
19. B. deferment
20. C. incidentally

TEST 9

DIRECTIONS: In each of the following tests in this part, select the letter of the one MISSPELLED word in each of the following groups of words. If no word is misspelled, select the last item, letter E (none misspelled). *PRINT THE LETTER OF THE CORRECT ANSWER IN THE SPACE AT THE RIGHT.*

1. A. irreparably   B. lovable   C. comparitively   1._____
   D. audible   E. *NONE MISSPELLED*

2. A. vilify   B. efflorescence   C. sarcophagus   2._____
   D. sacreligious   E. *NONE MISSPELLED*

3. A. picnicking   B. proceedure   C. hypocrisy   3._____
   D. seize   E. *NONE MISSPELLED*

4. A. discomfit   B. sapient   C. exascerbate   4._____
   D. sarsaparilla   E. *NONE MISSPELLED*

5. A. valleys   B. maintainance   C. abridgment   5._____
   D. reticence   E. *NONE MISSPELLED*

6. A. idylic   B. beneficent   C. singeing   6._____
   D. asterisk   E. *NONE MISSPELLED*

7. A. appropos   B. violoncello   C. peony   7._____
   D. mucilage   E. *NONE MISSPELLED*

8. A. caterpillar   B. silhouette   C. rhapsody   8._____
   D. frieze   E. *NONE MISSPELLED*

9. A. appendicitis   B. vestigeal   C. colonnade   9._____
   D. tortuous   E. *NONE MISSPELLED*

10. A. omlet   B. diphtheria   C. highfalutin   10._____
    D. miniature   E. *NONE MISSPELLED*

11. A. diorama   B. sustanance   C. disastrous   11._____
    D. conscious   E. *NONE MISSPELLED*

12. A. inelegible   B. irreplaceable   C. dissatisfied   12._____
    D. procedural   E. *NONE MISSPELLED*

13. A. contemptible   B. sacrilegious   C. proffessor   13._____
    D. privilege   E. *NONE MISSPELLED*

14. A. inoculate   B. diptheria   C. gladioli   14._____
    D. hypocrisy   E. *NONE MISSPELLED*

15. A. pessimism   B. ecstasy   C. furlough   15._____
    D. vulnerible   E. *NONE MISSPELLED*

16. A. supersede   B. moccasin   C. recondite   16._____
    D. rhythmical   E. *NONE MISSPELLED*

17. A. Adirondack   B. Phillipines   C. Czechoslovakia   17._____
    D. Cincinnati   E. *NONE MISSPELLED*

18.	A. weird	B. impromptu	C. guerrila	18.____
	D. spontaneously	E. *NONE MISSPELLED*		
19.	A. newstand	B. accidentally	C. tangible	19.____
	D. reservoir	E. *NONE MISSPELLED*		
20.	A. macaroni	B. mackerel	C. ukulele	20.____
	D. giutar	E. *NONE MISSPELLED*		

KEY (CORRECT ANSWERS)

1. C. comparatively
2. D. sacrilegious
3. B. procedure
4. C. exacerbate
5. B. maintenance
6. A. idyllic
7. A. apropos
8. E. None Misspelled
9. B. vestigial
10. A. omelet
11. B. sustenance
12. A. ineligible
13. C. professor
14. B. diphtheria
15. D. vulnerable
16. E. None Misspelled
17. B. Philippines
18. C. guerrilla
19. A. newsstand
20. D. guitar

TEST 10

DIRECTIONS: In each of the following tests in this part, select the letter of the one MIS-SPELLED word in each of the following groups of words. If no word is misspelled, select the last item, letter E (none misspelled). *PRINT THE LETTER OF THE CORRECT ANSWER IN THE SPACE AT THE RIGHT.*

1. A. rescission B. sacrament C. hypocricy 1.____
   D. salable E. *NONE MISSPELLED*

2. A. rhythm B. foreboding C. withal 2.____
   D. consciousness E. *NONE MISSPELLED*

3. A. noticeable B. drunkenness C. frolicked 3.____
   D. abcess E. *NONE MISSPELLED*

4. A. supersede B. canoeing C. exorbitant 4.____
   D. vigilance E. *NONE MISSPELLED*

5. A. idiosyncrasy B. pantomine C. isosceles 5.____
   D. wintry E. *NONE MISSPELLED*

6. A. numbskull B. indispensable C. fatiguing 6.____
   D. gluey E. *NONE MISSPELLED*

7. A. dryly B. egregious C. recommend 7.____
   D. irresistable' E. *NONE MISSPELLED*

8. A. unforgettable B. mackeral C. perseverance 8.____
   D. rococo E. *NONE MISSPELLED*

9. A. mischievous B. tyranical C. desiccate 9.____
   D. battalion E. *NONE MISSPELLED*

10. A. accede B. ninth C. abyssmal 10.____
    D. commonalty E. *NONE MISSPELLED*

11. A. resplendent B. colonnade C. harass 11.____
    D. mimicking E. *NONE MISSPELLED*

12. A. dilletante B. pusillanimous C. grievance 12.____
    D. cataclysm E. *NONE MISSPELLED*

13. A. anomaly B. connoisseur C. feasable 13.____
    D. stationery E. *NONE MISSPELLED*

14. A. ennervated B. rescission C. vacillate 14.____
    D. raucous E. *NONE MISSPELLED*

15. A. liquefy B. poniard C. truculant 15.____
    D. weird E. *NONE MISSPELLED*

16. A. existance B. lieutenant C. asinine 16.____
    D. parallelogram E. *NONE MISSPELLED*

17. A. protuberant B. nuisance C. instrumental 17.____
    D. resevoir E. *NONE MISSPELLED*

109

18.	A. sustenance D. clairvoyant	B. pedigree E. *NONE MISSPELLED*	C. supercillious	18.____
19.	A. commingle D. priviledge	B. bizarre E. *NONE MISSPELLED*	C. gauge	19.____
20.	A. analagous D. hindrance	B. irresistible E. *NONE MISSPELLED*	C. apparel	20.____

KEY (CORRECT ANSWERS)

1. C. hypocrisy
2. E. None Misspelled
3. D. abscess
4. E. None Misspelled
5. B. pantomime
6. A. numskull
7. D. irresistible
8. B. mackerel
9. B. tyrannical
10. C. abysmal
11. E. None Misspelled
12. A. dilettante
13. C. feasible
14. A. enervated
15. C. truculent
16. A. existence
17. D. reservoir
18. C. supercilious
19. D. privilege
20. A. analogous

TEST 11

DIRECTIONS: In each of the following tests in this part, select the letter of the one MISSPELLED word in each of the following groups of words. If no word is misspelled, select the last item, letter E (none misspelled). *PRINT THE LETTER OF THE CORRECT ANSWER IN THE SPACE AT THE RIGHT.*

1. A. impute B. imparshal C. immodest 1._____
   D. imminent E. *NONE MISSPELLED*

2. A. cover B. audit C. adege 2._____
   D. adder E. *NONE MISSPELLED*

3. A. promissory B. maturity C. severally 3._____
   D. accomodation E. *NONE MISSPELLED*

4. A. superintendant B. dependence C. dependents 4._____
   D. entrance E. *NONE MISSPELLED*

5. A. managable B. navigable C. passable 5._____
   D. laughable E. *NONE MISSPELLED*

6. A. tolerance B. circumference C. insurance 6._____
   D. dominance E. *NONE MISSPELLED*

7. A. diameter B. tangent C. paralell 7._____
   D. perimeter E. *NONE MISSPELLED*

8. A. providential B. personal C. accidental 8._____
   D. diagonel E. *NONE MISSPELLED*

9. A. ballast B. ballustrade C. allotment 9._____
   D. bourgeois E. *NONE MISSPELLED*

10. A. diverse B. pedantic C. mishapen 10._____
    D. transient E. *NONE MISSPELLED*

11. A. surgeon B. sturgeon C. luncheon 11._____
    D. stancheon E. *NONE MISSPELLED*

12. A. pariah B. estrang C. conceive 12._____
    D. puncilious E. *NONE MISSPELLED*

13. A. camouflage B. serviceable C. mischievious 13._____
    D. menace E. *NONE MISSPELLED*

14. A. forefeit B. halve C. hundredth 14._____
    D. illusion E. *NONE MISSPELLED*

15. A. filial B. arras C. pantomine 15._____
    D. filament E. *NONE MISSPELLED*

16. A. llama B. madrigal C. martinet 16._____
    D. laxitive E. *NONE MISSPELLED*

17. A. symtom B. serum C. antiseptic 17._____
    D. aromatic E. *NONE MISSPELLED*

18. A. erasable B. irascible C. audable 18.___
    D. laudable E. NONE MISSPELLED

19. A. heroes   B. folios   C. sopranos 19.___
    D. cargos   E. NONE MISSPELLED

20. A. latent   B. goddess   C. aisle   20.___
    D. whose   E. NONE MISSPELLED

KEY (CORRECT ANSWERS)

1. B. impartial
2. C. adage
3. D. accommodation
4. A. superintendent
5. A. manageable
6. E. None Misspelled
7. C. parallel
8. D. diagonal
9. B. balustrade
10. C. misshapen
11. D. stanchion
12. B. estrange
13. C. mischievous
14. A. forfeit
15. C. pantomime
16. D. laxative
17. A. symptom
18. C. audible
19. D. cargoes
20. E. None Misspelled

TEST 12

DIRECTIONS: In each of the following tests in this part, select the letter of the one MISSPELLED word in each of the following groups of words. If no word is misspelled, select the last item, letter E (none misspelled). *PRINT THE LETTER OF THE CORRECT ANSWER IN THE SPACE AT THE RIGHT.*

1. A. coconut B. bustling C. abducter 1._____
   D. naphtha E. *NONE MISSPELLED*

2. A. seriatim B. quadruped C. diphthong 2._____
   D. concensus E. *NONE MISSPELLED*

3. A. sanction B. propencity C. parabola 3._____
   D. despotic E. *NONE MISSPELLED*

4. A. circumstantial B. imbroglio C. coalesce 4._____
   D. ductill E. *NONE MISSPELLED*

5. A. spontaneous B. superlitive C. telepathy 5._____
   D. thesis E. *NONE MISSPELLED*

6. A. adobe B. apellate C. billion 6._____
   D. chiropody E. *NONE MISSPELLED*

7. A. combatant B. helium C. esprit de corps 7._____
   D. debillity E. *NONE MISSPELLED*

8. A. iota B. gopher C. demoralize 8._____
   D. culvert E. *NONE MISSPELLED*

9. A. invideous B. gourmand C. embryo 9._____
   D. despicable E. *NONE MISSPELLED*

10. A. dispeptic B. dromedary C. dormant 10._____
    D. duress E. *NONE MISSPELLED*

11. A. spiggot B. suffrage C. technology 11._____
    D. thermostat E. *NONE MISSPELLED*

12. A. aberration B. antropology C. bayou 12._____
    D. cashew E. *NONE MISSPELLED*

13. A. ricochet B. poncho C. oposum 13._____
    D. melee E. *NONE MISSPELLED*

14. A. semester B. quadrent C. penchant 14._____
    D. mustang E. *NONE MISSPELLED*

15. A. rhetoric B. polygimy C. optimum 15._____
    D. mendicant E. *NONE MISSPELLED*

16. A. labyrint B. hegira C. ergot 16._____
    D. debenture E. *NONE MISSPELLED*

17. A. solvant B. radioactive C. photostat 17._____
    D. nominative E. *NONE MISSPELLED*

18.	A. sporadic	B. excelsior	C. tenible	18.____
	D. thorax	E. *NONE MISSPELLED*		
19.	A. mischievous	B. bouillon	C. asinine	19.____
	D. alien	E. *NONE MISSPELLED*		
20.	A. sanguinery	B. prolix	C. harangue	20.____
	D. minutia	E. *NONE MISSPELLED*		

KEY (CORRECT ANSWERS)

1. C. abductor
2. D. consensus
3. B. propensity
4. D. ductile
5. B. superlative
6. B. appellate
7. D. debility
8. E. None Misspelled
9. A. invidious
10. A. dyspeptic
11. A. spigot
12. B. anthropology
13. C. opossum
14. B. quadrant
15. B. polygamy
16. A. labyrinth
17. A. solvent
18. C. tenable
19. E. None Misspelled
20. A. sanguinary

TEST 13

DIRECTIONS: In each of the following tests in this part, select the letter of the one MISSPELLED word in each of the following groups of words. If no word is misspelled, select the last item, letter E (none misspelled). *PRINT THE LETTER OF THE CORRECT ANSWER IN THE SPACE AT THE RIGHT.*

1. A. controvert B. cache C. auricle 1.____
   D. impromptu E. NONE MISSPELLED

2. A. labial B. heffer C. intrigue 2.____
   D. decagon E. NONE MISSPELLED

3. A. statistics B. syllable C. tenon 3.____
   D. tituler E. NONE MISSPELLED

4. A. lenient B. migraine C. embarras 4.____
   D. nepotism E. NONE MISSPELLED

5. A. lichen B. horoscope C. orthadox 5.____
   D. pageant E. NONE MISSPELLED

6. A. libretto B. humis C. fallacy 6.____
   D. dextrose E. NONE MISSPELLED

7. A. clinical B. alimoney C. bourgeois 7.____
   D. proverbial E. NONE MISSPELLED

8. A. dictator B. clipper C. braggadoccio 8.____
   D. assuage E. NONE MISSPELLED

9. A. reverence B. hydraulic C. felon 9.____
   D. diaphram E. NONE MISSPELLED

10. A. retrobution B. polyp C. optician 10.____
    D. mentor E. NONE MISSPELLED

11. A. resonant B. helicopter C. rejoicing 11.____
    D. decisive E. NONE MISSPELLED

12. A. renigade B. restitution C. faculty 12.____
    D. devise E. NONE MISSPELLED

13. A. solicitors B. gratuitous C. spherical 13.____
    D. crusible E. NONE MISSPELLED

14. A. spongy B. ramify C. pica 14.____
    D. noxtious E. NONE MISSPELLED

15. A. automaton B. cadence C. consummate 15.____
    D. ancillery E. NONE MISSPELLED

16. A. magnanimous B. iminent C. tonsillitis 16.____
    D. dowager E. NONE MISSPELLED

17. A. aerial B. apprehend C. bilinear 17.____
    D. transum E. NONE MISSPELLED

18. A. vacuum B. idiom C. veriety 18.____
    D. warbler E. *NONE MISSPELLED*

19. A. zephyr B. rarify C. physiology 19.____
    D. nonpareil E. *NONE MISSPELLED*

20. A. risque B. posterity C. opus 20.____
    D. meridian E. *NONE MISSPELLED*

KEY (CORRECT ANSWERS)

1. E. None Misspelled
2. B. heifer
3. D. titular
4. C. embarrass
5. C. orthodox
6. B. humus
7. B. alimony
8. C. braggadocio
9. D. diaphragm
10. A. retribution
11. E. None Misspelled
12. A. renegade
13. D. crucible
14. D. noxious
15. D. ancillary
16. B. imminent
17. D. transom
18. C. variety
19. B. rarefy
20. D. meridian

TEST 14

DIRECTIONS: In each of the following tests in this part, select the letter of the one MIS-SPELLED word in each of the following groups of words. If no word is misspelled, select the last item, letter E (none misspelled). *PRINT THE LETTER OF THE CORRECT ANSWER IN THE SPACE AT THE RIGHT.*

1. A. pygmy   B. seggregation   C. clayey   1.____
   D. homogeneous   E. *NONE MISSPELLED*

2. A. homeopathy   B. predelection   C. hindrance   2.____
   D. guillotine   E. *NONE MISSPELLED*

3. A. cumulative   B. dandelion   C. incission   3.____
   D. malpractice   E. *NONE MISSPELLED*

4. A. paradise   B. allegiance   C. frustrate   4.____
   D. impecunious   E. *NONE MISSPELLED*

5. A. licquor   B. mousse   C. exclamatory   5.____
   D. disciple   E. *NONE MISSPELLED*

6. A. lame   B. winesome   C. valvular   6.____
   D. unadvised   E. *NONE MISSPELLED*

7. A. Terre Haute   B. Cyrano de Bergerac   C. Stamboul   7.____
   D. Roosvelt   E. *NONE MISSPELLED*

8. A. perambulator   B. ruminate   C. litturgy   8.____
   D. staple   E. *NONE MISSPELLED*

9. A. hectic   B. inpregnate   C. otter   9.____
   D. muscat   E. *NONE MISSPELLED*

10. A. lighterage   B. lumbar   C. insurence   10.____
    D. monsoon   E. *NONE MISSPELLED*

11. A. lethal   B. iliterateness   C. manifold   11.____
    D. minuet   E. *NONE MISSPELLED*

12. A. forfeit   B. halve   C. hundredth   12.____
    D. illusion   E. *NONE MISSPELLED*

13. A. dissolute   B. conundrum   C. fallacious   13.____
    D. descrimination   E. *NONE MISSPELLED*

14. A. diva   B. codicile   C. expedient   14.____
    D. garrison   E. *NONE MISSPELLED*

15. A. filial   B. arras   C. pantomine   15.____
    D. filament   E. *NONE MISSPELLED*

16. A. inveigle   B. paraphenalia   C. archivist   16.____
    D. complexion   E. *NONE MISSPELLED*

17. A. dessicate   B. ambidextrous   C. meritorious   17.____
    D. revocable   E. *NONE MISSPELLED*

18. A. queue   B. isthmus   C. committal   18.____
    D. binnocular E. *NONE MISSPELLED*

19. A. changeable B. abbreviating C. regretable 19.____
    D. japanned   E. *NONE MISSPELLED*

20. A. Saskechewan B. Bismarck C. Albuquerque 20.____
    D. Apennines   E. *NONE MISSPELLED*

KEY (CORRECT ANSWERS)

1. B. segregation
2. B. predilection
3. C. incision
4. E. None Misspelled
5. A. liquor
6. B. winsome
7. D. Roosevelt
8. C. liturgy
9. B. impregnate
10. C. insurance
11. B. illiterateness
12. E. None Misspelled
13. D. discrimination
14. B. codicil
15. C. pantomime
16. B. paraphernalia
17. A. desiccate
18. D. binocular
19. C. regrettable
20. A. Saskatchewan

TEST 15

DIRECTIONS: In each of the following tests in this part, select the letter of the one MISSPELLED word in each of the following groups of words. If no word is misspelled, select the last item, letter E (none misspelled). *PRINT THE LETTER OF THE CORRECT ANSWER IN THE SPACE AT THE RIGHT.*

1. A. culinery B. millinery C. humpbacked D. improvise E. NONE MISSPELLED   1._____

2. A. Brittany B. embarrassment C. coifure D. leveled E. NONE MISSPELLED   2._____

3. A. minnion B. aborgine C. antagonism D. arabesque E. NONE MISSPELLED   3._____

4. A. tractible B. camouflage C. permanent D. dextrous E. NONE MISSPELLED   4._____

5. A. inequitous B. kilowatt C. weasel D. lunging E. NONE MISSPELLED   5._____

6. A. palatable B. odious C. motif D. Maltese E. NONE MISSPELLED   6._____

7. A. Beau Brummel B. Febuary C. Bedouin D. Damascus E. NONE MISSPELLED   7._____

8. A. llama B. madrigal C. illitive D. marlin E. NONE MISSPELLED   8._____

9. A. babboon B. dossier C. esplanade D. frontispiece E. NONE MISSPELLED   9._____

10. A. thrashing B. threshing C. atavism D. artifect E. NONE MISSPELLED   10._____

11. A. ballast B. ballustrade C. allotment D. bourgeois E. NONE MISSPELLED   11._____

12. A. amenuensis B. saccharine C. hippopotamus D. rhinoceros E. NONE MISSPELLED   12._____

13. A. maintenance B. bullion C. khaki D. libarian E. NONE MISSPELLED   13._____

14. A. diverse B. pedantic C. mishapen D. transient E. NONE MISSPELLED   14._____

15. A. exhilirate B. avaunt C. avocado D. avocation E. NONE MISSPELLED   15._____

16. A. narcotic B. flippancy C. daffodil D. narcisus E. NONE MISSPELLED   16._____

17. A. inflamation B. disfranchisement C. surmise D. adviser E. NONE MISSPELLED   17._____

18.	A. syphon D. collapsible		B. inquiry E. *NONE MISSPELLED*		C. shanghaied	18.____
19.	A. occassionally D. inveigh		B. antecedence E. *NONE MISSPELLED*		C. reprehensible	19.____
20.	A. crescendos D. impeccable		B. indispensible E. *NONE MISSPELLED*		C. mosquitoes	20.____

KEY (CORRECT ANSWERS)

1. A. culinary
2. C. coiffure
3. A. minion
4. A. tractable
5. A. iniquitous
6. E. None Misspelled
7. B. February
8. D. illative
9. A. baboon
10. D. artifact
11. B. balustrade
12. A. amanuensis
13. D. librarian
14. C. misshapen
15. A. exhilarate
16. D. narcissus
17. A. inflammation
18. E. None Misspelled
19. A. occasionally
20. B. indispensable

EXAMINATION SECTION
TEST 1

DIRECTIONS: Each question or incomplete statement is followed by several suggested answers or completions. Select the one that BEST answers the question or completes the statement. *PRINT THE LETTER OF THE CORRECT ANSWER IN THE SPACE AT THE RIGHT.*

1. Which of the following sentences is punctuated INCORRECTLY? 1.____
   A. Johnson said, "One tiny virus, Blanche, can multiply so fast that it will become 200 viruses in 25 minutes."
   B. With economic pressures hitting them from all sides, American farmers have become the weak link in the food chain.
   C. The degree to which this is true, of course, depends on the personalities of the people involved, the subject matter, and the atmosphere in general.
   D. "What loneliness, asked George Eliot, is more lonely than distrust?"

2. Which of the following sentences is punctuated INCORRECTLY? 2.____
   A. Based on past experiences, do you expect the plumber to show up late, not have the right parts, and overcharge you.
   B. When polled, however, the participants were most concerned that it be convenient.
   C. No one mentioned the flavor of the coffee, and no one seemed to care that china was used instead of plastic.
   D. As we said before, sometimes people view others as things; they don't see them as living, breathing beings like themselves.

3. Convention members travelled here from Kingston New York Pittsfield Massachusetts Bennington Vermont and Hartford Connecticut. 3.____
   How many commas should there be in the above sentence?
   A. 3   B. 4   C. 5   D. 6

4. Of the two speakers the one who spoke about human rights is more famous and more humble. 4.____
   How many commas should there be in the above sentence?
   A. 1   B. 2   C. 3   D. 4

5. Which sentence is punctuated INCORRECTLY? 5.____
   A. Five people voted no; two voted yes; one person abstained.
   B. Well, consider what has been said here today, but we won't make any promises.
   C. Anthropologists divide history into three major periods: the Stone Age, the Bronze Age, and the Iron Age.
   D. Therefore, we may create a stereotype about people who are unsuccessful; we may see them as lazy, unintelligent, or afraid of success.

6. Which sentence is punctuated INCORRECTLY?
   A. Studies have found that the unpredictability of customer behavior can lead to a great deal of stress, particularly if the behavior is unpleasant or if the employee has little control over it.
   B. If this degree of emotion and variation can occur in spectator sports, imagine the role that perceptions can play when there are real stakes involved.
   C. At other times, however hidden expectations may sabotage or severely damage an encounter without anyone knowing what happened.
   D. There are usually four issues to look for in a conflict: differences in values, goals, methods, and facts.

Questions 7-10.

DIRECTIONS: Questions 7 through 10 test your ability to distinguish between words that sound alike but are spelled differently and have different meanings. In the following groups of sentences, one of the underlined words is used incorrectly.

7. A. By accepting responsibility for their actions, managers promote trust.
   B. Dropping hints or making illusions to things that you would like changed sometimes leads to resentment.
   C. The entire unit loses respect for the manager and resents the reprimand.
   D. Many people are averse to confronting problems directly; they would rather avoid them.

8. A. What does this say about the effect our expectations have on those we supervise?
   B. In an effort to save time between 9 A.M. and 1 P.M., the staff members devised their own interpretation of what was to be done on these forms.
   C. The taskmaster's principal concern is for getting the work done; he or she is not concerned about the need or interests of employees.
   D. The advisor's main objective was increasing Angela's ability to invest her capitol wisely.

9. A. A typical problem is that people have to cope with the internal censer of their feelings.
   B. Sometimes, in their attempt to sound more learned, people speak in ways that are barely comprehensible.
   C. The council will meet next Friday to decide whether Abrams should continue as representative.
   D. His descent from grace was assured by that final word.

10. A. The doctor said that John's leg had to remain stationary or it would not heal properly.
    B. There is a city ordinance against parking too close to fire hydrants.
    C. Meyer's problem is that he is never discrete when talking about office politics.
    D. Mrs. Thatcher probably worked harder than any other British Prime Minister had ever worked.

Questions 11-20.

DIRECTIONS: For each of the following groups of sentences in Questions 11 through 20, select the sentence which is the BEST example of English usage and grammar.

11. A. She is a woman who, at age sixty, is distinctly attractive and cares about how they look.
    B. It was a seemingly impossible search, and no one knew the problems better than she.
    C. On the surface, they are all sweetness and light, but his morbid character is under it.
    D. The minicopier, designed to appeal to those who do business on the run like architects in the field or business travelers, weigh about four pounds.

11.____

12. A. Neither the administrators nor the union representative regret the decision to settle the disagreement.
    B. The plans which are made earlier this year were no longer being considered.
    C. I would have rode with him if I had known he was leaving at five.
    D. I don't know who she said had it.

12.____

13. A. Writing at a desk, the memo was handed to her for immediate attention.
    B. Carla didn't water Carl's plants this week, which she never does.
    C. Not only are they good workers, with excellent writing and speaking skills, and they get to the crux of any problem we hand them.
    D. We've noticed that this enthusiasm for undertaking new projects sometimes interferes with his attention to detail.

13.____

14. A. It's obvious that Nick offends people by being unruly, inattentive, and having no patience.
    B. Marcia told Genie that she would have to leave soon.
    C. Here are the papers you need to complete your investigation.
    D. Julio was startled by you're comment.

14.____

15. A. The new manager has done good since receiving her promotion, but her secretary has helped her a great deal.
    B. One of the personnel managers approached John and tells him that the client arrived unexpectedly.
    C. If somebody can supply us with the correct figures, they should do so immediately.
    D. Like zealots, advocates seek power because they want to influence the policies and actions of an organization.

15.____

16. A. Between you and me, Chris probably won't finish this assignment in time. 16.____
    B. Rounding the corner, the snack bar appeared before us.
    C. Parker's radical reputation made to the Supreme Court his appointment impossible.
    D. By the time we arrived, Marion finishes briefing James and returns to Hank's office.

17. A. As we pointed out earlier, the critical determinant of the success of middle managers is their ability to communicate well with others. 17.____
    B. The lecturer stated there wasn't no reason for bad supervision.
    C. We are well aware whose at fault in this instance.
    D. When planning important changes, it's often wise to seek the participation of others because employees often have much valuable ideas to offer.

18. A. Joan had ought to throw out those old things that were damaged when the roof leaked. 18.____
    B. I spose he'll let us know what he's decided when he finally comes to a decision.
    C. Carmen was walking to work when she suddenly realized that she had left her lunch on the table as she passed the market.
    D. Are these enough plants for your new office?

19. A. First move the lever forward, and then they should lift the ribbon casing before trying to take it out. 19.____
    B. Michael finished quickest than any other person in the office.
    C. There is a special meeting for we committee members today at 4 p.m.
    D. My husband is worried about our having to work overtime next week.

20. A. Another source of conflicts are individuals who possess very poor interpersonal skills. 20.____
    B. It is difficult for us to work with him on projects because these kinds of people are not interested in team building.
    C. Each of the departments was represented at the meeting.
    D. Poor boy, he never should of past that truck on the right.

Questions 21-28.

DIRECTIONS: In Questions 21 through 28, there may be a problem with English grammar or usage. If a problem does exist, select the letter that indicates the most effective change. If no problem exists, select Choice A.

21. He rushed her to the hospital and stayed with her, even though this took quite a bit of his time, he didn't charge her anything. 21.____
    A. No changes are necessary.
    B. Change even though to although
    C. Change the first comma to a period and capitalize even
    D. Change rushed to had rushed

22. Waiting that appears unfairly feels longer than waiting that seems justified.
    A. No changes are necessary.
    B. Change unfairly to unfair
    C. Change appears to seems
    D. Change longer to longest

    22.____

23. May be you and the person who argued with you will be able to reach an agreement.
    A. No changes are necessary
    B. Change will be to were
    C. Change argued with to had an argument with
    D. Change May be to Maybe

    23.____

24. Any one of them could of taken the file while you were having coffee.
    A. No changes are necessary
    B. Change any one to anyone
    C. Change of to have
    D. Change were having to were out having

    24.____

25. While people get jobs or move from poverty level to better paying employment, they stop receiving benefits and start paying taxes.
    A. No changes are necessary
    B. Change While to As
    C. Change stop to will stop
    D. Change get to obtain

    25.____

26. Maribeth's phone rang while talking to George about the possibility of their meeting Tom at three this afternoon.
    A. No changes are necessary
    B. Change their to her
    C. Move to George so that it follows Tom
    D. Change talking to she was talking

    26.____

27. According to their father, Lisa is smarter than Chris, but Emily is the smartest of the three sisters.
    A. No changes are necessary
    B. Change their to her
    C. Change is to was
    D. Make two sentences, changing the second comma to a period and omitting but

    27.____

28. Yesterday, Mark and he claim that Carl took Carol's ideas and used them inappropriately.
    A. No changes are necessary
    B. Change claim to claimed
    C. Change inappropriately to inappropriate
    D. Change Carol's to Carols'

    28.____

Questions 29-34.

DIRECTIONS: For each group of sentences in Questions 29 through 34, select the choice that represents the BEST editing of the problem sentence.

29. The managers expected employees to be at their desks at all times, but they would always be late or leave unannounced.
    A. The managers wanted employees to always be at their desks, but they would always be late or leave unannounced.
    B. Although the managers expected employees to be at their desks no matter what came up, they would always be late and leave without telling anyone.
    C. Although the managers expected employees to be at their desks at all times, the managers would always be late or leave without telling anyone.
    D. The managers expected the employee to never leave their desks, but they would always be late or leave without telling anyone.

29.____

30. The one who is department manager he will call you to discuss the problem tomorrow morning at 10 A.M.
    A. The one who is department manager will call you tomorrow morning at ten to discuss the problem.
    B. The department manager will call you to discuss the problem tomorrow at 10 A.M.
    C. Tomorrow morning at 10 A.M., the department manager will call you to discuss the problem.
    D. Tomorrow morning the department manager will call you to discuss the problem.

30.____

31. A conference on child care in the workplace the $200 cost of which to attend may be prohibitive to childcare workers who earn less than that weekly.
    A. A conference on child care in the workplace that costs $200 may be too expensive for childcare workers who earn less than that each week.
    B. A conference on child care in the workplace, the cost of which to attend is $200, may be prohibitive to childcare workers who earn less than that weekly.
    C. A conference on child care in the workplace who costs $200 may be too expensive for childcare workers who earn less than that a week.
    D. A conference on child care in the workplace which costs $200 may be too expensive to childcare workers who earn less than that on a weekly basis.

31.____

32. In accordance with estimates recently made, there are 40,000 to 50,000 nuclear weapons in our world today.
    A. Because of estimates recently, there are 40,000 to 50,000 nuclear weapons in the world today.
    B. In accordance with estimates made recently, there are 40,000 to 50,000 nuclear weapons in the world today.

32.____

C. According to estimates made recently, there are 40,000 to 50,000 weapons in the world today.
D. According to recent estimates, there are 40,000 to 50,000 nuclear weapons in the world today.

33. Motivation is important in problem solving, but they say that excessive motivation can inhibit the creative process. 33._____
    A. Motivation is important in problem solving, but, as they say, too much of it can inhibit the creative process.
    B. Motivation is important in problem solving and excessive motivation will inhibit the creative process.
    C. Motivation is important in problem solving, but excessive motivation can inhibit the creative process.
    D. Motivation is important in problem solving because excessive motivation can inhibit the creative process.

34. In selecting the best option calls for consulting with all the people that are involved in it. 34._____
    A. In selecting the best option consulting with all people concerned with it.
    B. Calling for the best option, we consulted all the affected people.
    C. We called all the people involved to select the best option.
    D. To be sure of selecting the best option, one should consult all the people involved.

35. There are a number of problems with the following letter. From the options below, select the version that is MOST in accordance with standard business style, tone, and form. 35._____

    Dear Sir:

    We are so sorry that we have had to backorder your order for 15,000 widgets and 2,300 whatzits for such a long time. We have been having incredibly bad luck lately. When your order first came in no one could get to it because my secretary was out with the flu and her replacement didn't know what she was doing, then there was the dock strike in Cucamonga which held things up for awhile, and then it just somehow got lost. We think it may have fallen behind the radiator.
    We are happy to say that all these problems have been taken care of, we are caught up on supplies, and we should have the stuff to you soon, in the near future—about two weeks. You may not believe us after everything you've been through with us, but it's true.
    We'll let you know as soon as we have a secure date for delivery. Thank you so much for continuing to do business with us after all the problems this probably has caused you.

    Yours very sincerely,
    Rob Barker

8 (#1)

A. Dear Sir:

    We are so sorry that we have had to backorder your order for 15,000 widgets and 2,300 whatzits. We have been having problems with staff lately and the dock strike hasn't helped anything.
    We are happy to say that all these problems have been taken care of. I've told my secretary to get right on it, and we should have the stuff to you soon. Thank you so much for continuing to do business with us after all the problems this must have caused you.
    We'll let you know as soon as we have a secure date for delivery.

Sincerely,
Rob Barker

B. Dear Sir:

    We regret that we haven't been able to fill your order for 15,000 widgets and 2,300 whatzits in a timely fashion.
    We'll let you know as soon as we have a secure date for delivery.

Sincerely,
Rob Barker

C. Dear Sir:

    We are so very sorry that we haven't been able to fill your order for 15,000 widgets and 2,300 whatzits. We have been having incredibly bad luck lately, but things are much better now.
    Thank you so much for bearing with us through all of this. We'll let you know as soon as we have a secure date for delivery.

Sincerely,
Rob Barker

D. Dear Sir:

    We are very sorry that we haven't been able to fill your order for 15,000 widgets and 2,300 whatzits. Due to unforeseen difficulties, we have had to back-order your request. At this time, supplies have caught up to demand, and we foresee a delivery date within the next two weeks.
    We'll let you know as soon as we have a secure date for delivery. Thank you for your patience.

Sincerely,
Rob Barker

KEY (CORRECT ANSWERS)

1. D	11. B	21. C	31. A
2. A	12. D	22. B	32. D
3. B	13. D	23. D	33. C
4. A	14. C	24. C	34. D
5. B	15. D	25. B	35. D
6. C	16. A	26. D	
7. B	17. A	27. A	
8. D	18. D	28. B	
9. A	19. D	29. C	
10. C	20. C	30. B	

CLERICAL ABILITIES
EXAMINATION SECTION
TEST 1

DIRECTIONS: Each question or incomplete statement is followed by several suggested answers or completions. Select the one that BEST answers the question or completes the statement. *PRINT THE LETTER OF THE CORRECT ANSWER IN THE SPACE AT THE RIGHT.*

Questions 1-4.

DIRECTIONS: Questions 1 through 4 are to be answered on the basis of the information given below.

The most commonly used filing system and the one that is easiest to learn is alphabetical filing. This involves putting records in an A to Z order, according to the letters of the alphabet. The name of a person is filed by using the following order: first, the surname or last name; second, the first name; third, the middle name or middle initial. For example, *Henry C. Young* is filed under *Y* and thereafter under *Young, Henry C.* The name of a company is filed in the same way. For example, *Long Cabinet Co.* is filed under *L* while *John T. Long Cabinet Co.* is filed under *L* and thereafter under *Long, John T. Cabinet Co.*

1. The one of the following which lists the names of persons in the CORRECT alphabetical order is:
   A. Mary Carrie, Helen Carrol, James Carson, John Carter
   B. James Carson, Mary Carrie, John Carter, Helen Carrol
   C. Helen Carrol, James Carson, John Carter, Mary Carrie
   D. John Carter, Helen Carrol, Mary Carrie, James Carson

1.____

2. The one of the following which lists the names of persons in the CORRECT alphabetical order is:
   A. Jones, John C.; Jones, John A.; Jones, John P.; Jones, John K.
   B. Jones, John P.; Jones, John K.; Jones, John C.; Jones, John A.
   C. Jones, John A.; Jones, John C.; Jones, John K.; Jones, John P.
   D. Jones, John K.; Jones, John C.; Jones, John A.; Jones, John P.

2.____

3. The one of the following which lists the names of the companies in the CORRECT alphabetical order is:
   A. Blane Co., Blake Co., Block Co., Blear Co.
   B. Blake Co., Blane Co., Blear Co., Block Co.
   C. Block Co., Blear Co., Blane Co., Blake Co.
   D. Blear Co., Blake Co., Blane Co., Block Co.

3.____

4. You are to return to the file an index card on *Barry C. Wayne Materials and Supplies Co.*
   Of the following, the CORRECT alphabetical group that you should return the index card to is
   A. A to G   B. H to M   C. N to S   D. T to Z

Questions 5-10.

DIRECTIONS: In each of Questions 5 through 10, the names of four people are given. For each question, choose as your answer the one of the four names given which should be filed FIRST according to the usual system of alphabetical filing of names, as described in the following paragraph.

In filing names, you must start with the last name. Names are filed in order of the first letter of the last name, then the second letter, etc. Therefore, BAILY would be filed before BROWN, which would be filed before COLT. A name with fewer letters of the same type comes first, i.e., Smith before Smithe. If the last names are the same, the names are filed alphabetically by the first name. If the first name is an initial, a name with an initial would come before a first name that starts with the same letter as the initial. Therefore, I. BROWN would come before IRA BROWN. Finally, if both last name and first name are the same, the name would be filed alphabetically by the middle name, once again an initial coming before a middle name which starts with the same letter as the initial. If there is no middle name at all, the name would come before those with middle initials or names.

SAMPLE QUESTION:
    A. Lester Daniels
    B. William Dancer
    C. Nathan Danzig
    D. Dan Lester

The last names beginning with D are filed before the last name beginning with L. Since DANIELS, DANCER, and DANZIG all begin with the same three letters, you must look at the fourth letter of the last name to determine which name should be filed first. C comes before I or Z in the alphabet, so DANCER is filed before DANIELS or DANZIG. Therefore, the answer to the above sample question is B.

5.   A. Scott Biala
       B. Mary Byala
       C. Martin Baylor
       D. Francis Bauer

6.   A. Howard J. Black
       B. Howard Black
       C. J. Howard Black
       D. John H. Black

7.   A. Theodora Garth Kingston
       B. Theadore Barth Kingston
       C. Thomas Kingston
       D. Thomas T. Kingston

8. A. Paulette Mary Huerta
   B. Paul M. Huerta
   C. Paulette L. Huerta
   D. Peter A. Huerta

8.____

9. A. Martha Hunt Morgan
   B. Martin Hunt Morgan
   C. Mary H. Morgan
   D. Martine H. Morgan

9.____

10. A. James T. Meerschaum
    B. James M. Mershum
    C. James F. Mearshaum
    D. James N. Meshum

10.____

Questions 11-14.

DIRECTIONS: Questions 11 through 14 are to be answered SOLELY on the basis of the following information.

You are required to file various documents in file drawers which are labeled according to the following pattern:

DOCUMENTS

MEMOS		LETTERS	
File	Subject	File	Subject
84PM1	(A-L)	84PC1	(A-L)
84PM2	(M-Z)	84PC2	(M-Z)

REPORTS		INQUIRIES	
File	Subject	File	Subject
84PR1	(A-L)	84PQ1	(A-L)
84PR2	(M-Z)	84PQ2	(M-Z)

11. A letter dealing with a burglary should be filed in the drawer labeled
    A. 84PM1   B. 84PC1   C. 84PR1   D. 84PQ2

11.____

12. A report on Statistics should be found in the drawer labeled
    A. 84PM1   B. 84PC2   C. 84PR2   D. 84PQS

12.____

13. An inquiry is received about parade permit procedures. It should be filed in the drawer labeled
    A. 84PM2   B. 84PC1   C. 84PR1   D. 84PQ2

13.____

14. A police officer has a question about a robbery report you filed. You should pull this file from the drawer labeled
    A. 84PM1   B. 84PM2   C. 84PR1   D. 84PR2

14.____

4 (#1)

Questions 15-22.

DIRECTIONS: Each of Questions 15 through 22 consists of four or six numbered names. For each question, choose the option (A, B, C, or D) which indicates the order in which the names should be filed in accordance with the following filing instructions:
- File alphabetically according to last name, then first name, then middle initial.
- File according to each successive letter within a name.
- When comparing two names in which the letters in the longer name are identical to the corresponding letters in the shorter name, the shorter name is filed first.
- When the last names are the same, initials are always filed before names beginning with the same letter.

15. I.   Ralph Robinson
     II. Alfred Ross
     III. Luis Robles
     IV. James Roberts

   The CORRECT filing sequence for the above names should be
     A. IV, II, I, III   B. I, IV, III, II   C. III, IV, I, II   D. IV, I, III, II

16. I.   Irwin Goodwin
     II. Inez Gonzalez
     III. Irene Goodman
     IV. Ira S. Goodwin
     V.   Ruth I. Goldstein
     VI. M.B. Goodman

   The CORRECT filing sequence for the above names should be
     A. V, II, I, IV, III, VI   B. V, II, VI, III, IV, I
     C. V, II, III, VI, IV, I   D. V, II, III, VI, I, IV

17. I.   George Allan
     II. Gregory Allen
     III. Gary Allen
     IV. George Allen

   The CORRECT filing sequence for the above names should be
     A. IV, III, I, II   B. I, IV, II, III   C. III, IV, I, II   D. I, III, IV, II

18. I. Simon Kauffman
     II. Leo Kaufman
     III. Robert Kaufmann
     IV. Paul Kauffmann

     The CORRECT filing sequence for the above names should be
     A. I, IV, II, III   B. II, IV, III, I   C. III, II, IV, I   D. I, II, III, IV

19. I. Roberta Williams
     II. Robin Wilson
     III. Roberta Wilson
     IV. Robin Williams

     The CORRECT filing sequence for the above names should be
     A. III, II, IV, I   B. I, IV, III, II   C. I, II, III, IV   D. III, I, II, IV

20. I. Lawrence Shultz
     II. Albert Schultz
     III. Theodore Schwartz
     IV. Thomas Schwarz
     V. Alvin Schultz
     VI. Leonard Shultz

     The CORRECT filing sequence for the above names should be
     A. II, V, III, IV, I, VI   B. IV, III, V, I, II, VI
     C. II, V, I, VI, III, IV   D. I, VI, II, V, III, IV

21. I. McArdle
     II. Mayer
     III. Maletz
     IV. McNiff
     V. Meyer
     VI. MacMahon

     The CORRECT filing sequence for the above names should be
     A. I, IV, VI, III, II, V   B. II, I, IV, VI, III, V
     C. VI, III, II, I, IV, V   D. VI, III, II, V, I, IV

22. I. Jack E. Johnson
     II. R.H. Jackson
     III. Bertha Jackson
     IV. J.T. Johnson
     V. Ann Johns
     VI. John Jacobs

     The CORRECT filing sequence for the above names should be
     A. II, III, VI, V, IV, I   B. III, II, VI, V, IV, I
     C. VI, II, III, I, V, IV   D. III, II, VI, IV, V, I

Questions 23-30.

DIRECTIONS: The code table below shows 10 letters with matching numbers. For each question, there are three sets of letters. Each set of letters is followed by a set of numbers which may or may not match their correct letter according to the code table. For each question, check all three sets of letters and numbers and mark your answer:
    A. if no pairs are correctly matched
    B. if only one pair is correctly matched
    C. if only two pairs are correctly matched
    D. if all three pairs are correctly matched

CODE TABLE

T	M	V	D	S	P	R	G	B	H
1	2	3	4	5	6	7	8	9	0

SAMPLE QUESTION: TMVDSP – 123456
RGBHTM – 789011
DSPRGB – 256789

In the sample question above, the first set of numbers correctly match its set of letters. But the second and third pairs contain mistakes. In the second pair, M is correctly matched with number 1. According to the code table, letter M should be correctly matched with number 2. In the third pair, the letter D is incorrectly matched with number 2. According to the code table, letter D should be correctly matched with number 4. Since only one of the pairs is correctly matched, the answer to this sample question is B.

23. RSBMRM – 759262
     GDSRVH – 845730
     VDBRTM - 349713

24. TGVSDR – 183247
     SMHRDP – 520647
     TRMHSR - 172057

25. DSPRGM – 456782
     MVDBHT – 234902
     HPMDBT - 062491

26. BVPTRD – 936184
     GDPHMB – 807029
     GMRHMV – 827032

27. MGVRSH – 283750
     TRDMBS – 174295
     SPRMGV - 567283

23._____

24._____

25._____

26._____

27._____

28. SGBSDM – 489542
    MGHPTM – 290612
    MPBMHT - 269301

29. TDPBHM – 146902
    VPBMRS – 369275
    GDMBHM - 842902

30. MVPTBV – 236194
    PDRTMB – 47128
    BGTMSM - 981232

28.____

29.____

30.____

KEY (CORRECT ANSWERS)

1.	A	11.	B	21.	C
2.	C	12.	C	22.	B
3.	B	13.	D	23.	B
4.	D	14.	D	24.	B
5.	D	15.	D	25.	C
6.	B	16.	C	26.	A
7.	B	17.	D	27.	D
8.	B	18.	A	28.	A
9.	A	19.	B	29.	D
10.	C	20.	A	30.	A

TEST 2

DIRECTIONS: Each question or incomplete statement is followed by several suggested answers or completions. Select the one that BEST answers the question or completes the statement. *PRINT THE LETTER OF THE CORRECT ANSWER IN THE SPACE AT THE RIGHT.*

Questions 1-10.

DIRECTIONS: Questions 1 through 10 each consists of two columns, each containing four lines of names, numbers and/or addresses. For each question, compare the lines in Column I with the lines in Column II to see if they match exactly, and mark your answer A, B, C, or D, according to the following instructions:
    A. all four lines match exactly
    B. only three lines match exactly
    C. only two lines match exactly
    D. only one line matches exactly

COLUMN I   COLUMN II

1. I. Earl Hodgson   Earl Hodgson
    II. 1409870   1408970
    III. Shore Ave.   Schore Ave.
    IV. Macon Rd.   Macon Rd.

2. I. 9671485   9671485
    II. 470 Astor Court   470 Astor Court
    III. Halprin, Phillip   Halperin, Phillip
    IV. Frank D. Poliseo   Frank D. Poliseo

3. I. Tandem Associates   Tandom Associates
    II. 144-17 Northern Blvd.   144-17 Northern Blvd.
    III. Alberta Forchi   Albert Forchi
    IV. Kings Park, NY 10751   Kings Point, NY 10751

4. I. Bertha C. McCormack   Bertha C. McCormack
    II. Clayton, MO   Clayton, MO
    III. 976-4242   976-4242
    IV. New City, NY 10951   New City, NY 10951

5. I. George C. Morill   George C. Morrill
    II. Columbia, SC 29201   Columbia, SD 29201
    III. Louis Ingham   Louis Ingham
    IV. 3406 Forest Ave.   3406 Forest Ave.

6. I. 506 S. Elliott Pl.   506 S. Elliott Pl.
    II. Herbert Hall   Hurbert Hall
    III. 4712 Rockaway Pkway   4712 Rockaway Pkway
    IV. 169 E. 7 St.   169 E. 7 St.

7. I.   345 Park Ave.   345 Park Pl.   7.____
    II. Colman Oven Corp.   Coleman Oven Corp.
    III. Robert Conte   Robert Conti
    IV. 6179846   6179846

8. I.   Grigori Schierber   Grigori Schierber   8.____
    II. Des Moines, Iowa   Des Moines, Iowa
    III. Gouverneur Hospital   Gouverneur Hospital
    IV. 91-35 Cresskill Pl.   91-35 Cresskill Pl.

9. I.   Jeffery Janssen   Jeffrey Janssen   9.____
    II. 8041071   8041071
    III. 40 Rockefeller Plaza   40 Rockafeller Plaza
    IV. 407 6 St.   406 7 St.

10. I.   5971996   5871996   10.____
    II. 3113 Knickerbocker Ave.   31123 Knickerbocker Ave.
    III. 8434 Boston Post Rd.   8424 Boston Post Rd.
    IV. Penn Station   Penn Station

Questions 11-14.

DIRECTIONS: Questions 11 through 14 are to be answered by looking at the four groups of names and addresses listed below (I, II, III, and IV), and then finding out the number of groups that have their corresponding numbered lies exactly the same.

	GROUP I	GROUP II
Line 1.	Richmond General Hospital	Richman General Hospital
Line 2.	Geriatric Clinic	Geriatric Clinic
Line 3.	3975 Paerdegat St.	3975 Peardegat St.
Line 4.	Loudonville, New York 11538	Londonville, New York 11538

	GROUP III	GROUP IV
Line 1.	Richmond General Hospital	Richmend General Hospital
Line 2.	Geriatric Clinic	Geriatric Clinic
Line 3.	3795 Paerdegat St.	3975 Paerdegat St.
Line 4.	Loudonville, New York 11358	Loudonville, New York 11538

1. In how many groups is line one exactly the same?   11.____
       A. Two   B. Three   C. Four   D. None

12. In how many groups is line two exactly the same?   12.____
       A. Two   B. Three   C. Four   D. None

13. In how many groups is line three exactly the same?   13.____
       A. Two   B. Three   C. Four   D. None

14. In how many groups is line four exactly the same? 14.____
    A. Two   B. Three   C. Four   D. None

Questions 15-18.

DIRECTIONS: Each of Questions 15 through 18 has two lists of names and addresses. Each list contains three sets of names and addresses. Check each of the three sets in the list on the right to see if they are the same as the corresponding set in the list on the left. Mark your answers:
   A. if none of the sets in the right list are the same as those in the left list
   B. if only one of the sets in the right list is the same as those in the left list
   C. if only two of the sets in the right list are the same as those in the left list
   D. if all three sets in the right list are the same as those in the left list

15. Mary T. Berlinger   Mary T. Berlinger   15.____
    2351 Hampton St.   2351 Hampton St.
    Monsey, N.Y. 20117   Monsey, N.Y. 20117

    Eduardo Benes   Eduardo Benes
    483 Kingston Avenue   473 Kingston Avenue
    Central Islip, N.Y. 11734   Central Islip, N.Y. 11734

    Alan Carrington Fuchs   Alan Carrington Fuchs
    17 Gnarled Hollow Road   17 Gnarled Hollow Road
    Los Angeles, CA 91635   Los Angeles, CA 91685

16. David John Jacobson   David John Jacobson   16.____
    178 34 St. Apt. 4C   178 53 St. Apt. 4C
    New York, N.Y. 00927   New York, N.Y. 00927

    Ann-Marie Calonella   Ann-Marie Calonella
    7243 South Ridge Blvd.   7243 South Ridge Blvd.
    Bakersfield, CA 96714   Bakersfield, CA 96714

    Pauline M. Thompson   Pauline M. Thomson
    872 Linden Ave.   872 Linden Ave.
    Houston, Texas 70321   Houston, Texas 70321

17. Chester LeRoy Masterton   Chester LeRoy Masterson   17.____
    152 Lacy Rd.   152 Lacy Rd.
    Kankakee, Ill. 54532   Kankakee, Ill. 54532

    William Maloney   William Maloney
    S. LaCrosse Pla.   S. LaCross Pla.
    Wausau, Wisconsin 52136   Wausau, Wisconsin 52146

    Cynthia V. Barnes   Cynthia V. Barnes
    16 Pines Rd.   16 Pines Rd.
    Greenpoint, Miss. 20376   Greenpoint,, Miss. 20376

4 (#2)

18. Marcel Jean Frontenac Marcel Jean Frontenac 18.____
    8 Burton On The Water 6 Burton On The Water
    Calender, Me. 01471   Calender, Me. 01471

    J. Scott Marsden   J. Scott Marsden
    174 S. Tipton St.   174 Tipton St.
    Cleveland, Ohio   Cleveland, Ohio

    Lawrence T. Haney   Lawrence T. Haney
    171 McDonough St.   171 McDonough St.
    Decatur, Ga. 31304   Decatur, Ga. 31304

Questions 19-26.

DIRECTIONS: Each of Questions 19 through 26 has two lists of numbers. Each list contains three sets of numbers. Check each of the three sets in the list on the right to see if they are the same as the corresponding set in the list on the left. Mark your answers:
- A. if none of the sets in the right list are the same as those in the left list
- B. if only one of the sets in the right list is the same as those in the left list
- C. if only two of the sets in the right list are the same as those in the left list
- D. if all three sets in the right list are the same as those in the left lists

19. 7354183476   7354983476   19.____
    4474747744   4474747774
    5791430231   57914302311

20. 7143592185   7143892185   20.____
    8344517699   8344518699
    9178531263   9178531263

21. 2572114731   257214731   21.____
    8806835476   8806835476
    8255831246   8255831246

22. 331476853821   331476858621   22.____
    6976658532996   6976655832996
    3766042113715   3766042113745

23. 8806663315   88066633115   23.____
    74477138449   74477138449
    211756663666   211756663666

141

24. 990006966996 53022219743 4171171117717	99000696996 53022219843 4171171177717	24._____
25. 24400222433004 5300030055000355 20000075532002022	24400222433004 5300030055500355 20000075532002022	25._____
26. 6111666406600001116 7111300117001100733 26666446664476518	61116664066001116 7111300117001100733 26666446664476518	26._____

Questions 27-30.

DIRECTIONS: Questions 27 through 30 are to be answered by picking the answer which is in the correct numerical order, from the lowest number to the highest number, in each question.

27. A. 44533, 44518, 44516, 44547
    B. 44516, 44518, 44533, 44547
    C. 44547, 44533, 44518, 44516
    D. 44518, 44516, 44547, 44533

27._____

28. A. 95587, 95593, 95601, 95620
    B. 95601, 95620, 95587, 95593
    C. 95593, 95587, 95601. 95620
    D. 95620, 95601, 95593, 95587

28._____

29. A. 232212, 232208, 232232, 232223
    B. 232208, 232223, 232212, 232232
    C. 232208, 232212, 232223, 232232
    D. 232223, 232232, 232208, 232208

29._____

30. A. 113419, 113521, 113462, 113462
    B. 113588, 113462, 113521, 113419
    C. 113521, 113588, 113419, 113462
    D. 113419, 113462, 113521, 113588

30._____

KEY (CORRECT ANSWERS)

1.	C	11.	A	21.	C
2.	B	12.	C	22.	A
3.	D	13.	A	23.	D
4.	A	14.	A	24.	A
5.	C	15.	C	25.	C
6.	B	16.	B	26.	C
7.	D	17.	B	27.	B
8.	A	18.	B	28.	A
9.	D	19.	B	29.	C
10.	C	20.	B	30.	D

ARITHMETICAL REASONING
EXAMINATION SECTION
TEST 1

DIRECTIONS: Each question or incomplete statement is followed by several suggested answers or completions. Select the one that BEST answers the question or completes the statement. *PRINT THE LETTER OF THE CORRECT ANSWER IN THE SPACE AT THE RIGHT.*

1. If a secretary answered 28 phone calls and typed the addresses for 112 credit statements in one morning, what is the RATIO of phone calls answered to credit statements typed for that period of time?

    A. 1:4 B. 1:7 C. 2:3 D. 3:5

    1._____

2. According to a suggested filing system, no more than 10 folders should be filed behind any one file guide and from 15 to 25 file guides should be used in each file drawer for easy finding and filing.
   The MAXIMUM number of folders that a five-drawer file cabinet can hold to allow easy finding and filing is

    A. 550 B. 750 C. 1,100 D. 1,250

    2._____

3. An employee had a starting salary of $19,353. He received a salary increase at the end of each year, and at the end of the seventh year his salary was $25,107.
   What was his AVERAGE annual increase in salary over these seven years?

    A. $765 B. $807 C. $822 D. $858

    3._____

4. The 55 typists and 28 senior clerks in a certain agency were paid a total of $1,457,400 in salaries in 2005.
   If the average annual salary of a typist was $16,800, the average annual salary of a senior clerk was

    A. $19,050 B. $19,950 C. $20,100 D. $20,250

    4._____

5. A typist has been given a three-page report to type. She has finished typing the first two pages. The first page has 283 words, and the second page has 366 words.
   If the total report consists of 954 words, how many words will she have to type on the third page of the report?

    A. 202 B. 287 C. 305 D. 313

    5._____

6. In one day, Clerk A processed 30% more forms than Clerk B, and Clerk C processed 1 1/4 as many forms as Clerk A.
   If Clerk B processed 40 forms, how many more forms were processed by Clerk C than Clerk B?

    A. 12 B. 13 C. 21 D. 25

    6._____

7. A clerk who earns a gross salary of $678 every 2 weeks has the following deductions taken from her paycheck: 15% for city, state, and federal taxes; 2 1/2% for Social Security; $1.95 for health insurance; and $9.00 for union dues.
The amount of her take-home pay is

   A. $429.60　　B. $468.60　　C. $497.40　　D. $548.40

8. In 2002, an agency spent $400 to buy pencils at a cost of $1.00 a dozen.
If the agency used 3/4 of these pencils in 2002 and used the same number of pencils in 2003, how many more pencils did it have to buy to have enough pencils for all of 2003?

   A. 1,200　　B. 2,400　　C. 3,600　　D. 4,800

9. A clerk who worked in Agency X earned the following salaries: $15,105 the first year, $15,750 the second year, and $16,440 the third year. Another clerk who worked in Agency Y for three years earned $15,825 a year for two years and $16,086 the third year. The DIFFERENCE between the average salaries received by both clerks over a three-year period is

   A. $147　　B. $153　　C. $261　　D. $423

10. An employee who works more than 40 hours in any week receives overtime payment for the extra hours at time and one-half (1 1/2 times) his hourly rate of pay. An employee who earns $13.60 an hour works a total of 45 hours during a certain week.
His TOTAL pay for that week would be

    A. $564.40　　B. $612.00　　C. $646.00　　D. $824.00

11. Suppose that the amount of money spent for supplies in 2006 for a division in a city department was $156,500. This represented an increase of 12% over the amount spent for supplies for this division in 2005.
The amount of money spent for supplies for this division in 2005 was MOST NEARLY

    A. $139,730　　B. $137,720　　C. $143,460　　D. $138,720

12. Suppose that a group of five clerks have been assigned to insert 24,000 letters into envelopes. The clerks perform this work at the following rates of speed: Clerk A, 1,100 letters an hour; Clerk B, 1,450 letters an hour; Clerk C, 1,200 letters an hour; Clerk D, 1,300 letters an hour; Clerk E, 1,250 letters an hour. At the end of two hours of work, Clerks C and D are assigned to another task.
From the time that Clerks C and D were taken off the assignment, the number of hours required for the remaining clerks to complete this assignment is

    A. less than 3 hours
    B. 3 hours
    C. more than 3 hours, but less than 4 hours
    D. more than 4 hours

13. The number 60 is 40% of

    A. 24　　B. 84　　C. 96　　D. 150

14. If 3/8 of a number is 96, the number is

    A. 132　　B. 36　　C. 256　　D. 156

15. A city department uses an average of 25 20-cent, 35 30-cent, and 350 40-cent postage stamps each day.
    The TOTAL cost of stamps used by the department in a five-day period is

    A. $29.50   B. $155.50   C. $290.50   D. $777.50

16. A city department issued 12,000 applications in 2000. The number of applications that the department issued in 1998 was 25% greater than the number it issued in 2000.
    If the department issued 10% fewer applications in 1996 than it did in 1998, the number it issued in 1996 was

    A. 16,500   B. 13,500   C. 9,900   D. 8,100

17. A clerk can add 40 columns of figures an hour by using an adding machine and 20 columns of figures an hour without using an adding machine.
    The TOTAL number of hours it would take him to add 200 columns if he does 3/5 of the work by machine and the rest without the machine is

    A. 6   B. 7   C. 8   D. 9

18. In 1997, a city department bought 500 dozen pencils at $1.20 per dozen. In 2000, only 75 percent as many pencils were bought as were bought in 1997, but the price was 20 percent higher than the 1997 price. The TOTAL cost of the pencils bought in 2000 was

    A. $540   B. $562.50   C. $720   D. $750

19. A clerk is assigned to check the accuracy of the entries on 490 forms. He checks 40 forms an hour. After working one hour on this task, he is joined by another clerk, who checks these forms at the rate of 35 an hour.
    The TOTAL number of hours required to do the entire assignment is

    A. 5   B. 6   C. 7   D. 8

20. Assume that there are a total of 420 employees in a city agency. Thirty percent of the employees are clerks, and 1/7 are typists.
    The DIFFERENCE between the number of clerks and the number of typists is

    A. 126   B. 66   C. 186   D. 80

21. Assume that a duplicating machine produces copies of a bulletin at a cost of 2 cents per copy. The machine produces 120 copies of the bulletin per minute.
    If the cost of producing a certain number of copies was $12, how many minutes of operation did it take the machine to produce this number of copies?

    A. 5   B. 2   C. 10   D. 6

22. An assignment is completed by 32 clerks in 22 days. Assuming that all the clerks work at the same rate of speed, the number of clerks that would be needed to complete this assignment in 16 days is

    A. 27   B. 38   C. 44   D. 52

23. A department head hired a total of 60 temporary employees to handle a seasonal increase in the department's workload. The following lists the number of temporary employees hired, their rates of pay, and the duration of their employment:
    One-third of the total were hired as clerks, each at the rate of $27,500 a year, for two months.
    30 percent of the total were hired as office machine operators, each at the rate of $31,500 a year, for four months.
    22 stenographers were hired, each at the rate of $30,000 a year, for three months.
    The total amount paid to these temporary employees was MOST NEARLY

    A. $1,780,000
    B. $450,000
    C. $650,000
    D. $390,000

24. Assume that there are 2,300 employees in a city agency. Also, assume that five percent of these employees are accountants, that 80 percent of the accountants have college degrees, and that one-half of the accountants who have college degrees have five years of experience. Then, the number of employees in the agency who are accountants with college degrees and five years of experience is

    A. 46   B. 51   C. 460   D. 920

25. Assume that the regular 8-hour working day of a laborer is from 8 A.M. to 5 P.M., with an hour off for lunch. He earns a regular hourly rate of pay for these 8 hours and is paid at the rate of time-and-a-half for each hour worked after his regular working day.
    If, on a certain day, he works from 8 A.M. to 6 P.M., with an hour off for lunch, and earns $171, his regular hourly rate of pay is

    A. $16.30   B. $17.10   C. $18.00   D. $19.00

KEY (CORRECT ANSWERS)

1. A
2. D
3. C
4. A
5. C
6. D
7. D
8. B
9. A
10. C

11. A
12. B
13. D
14. C
15. D
16. B
17. B
18. A
19. C
20. B

21. A
22. C
23. B
24. A
25. C

SOLUTIONS TO PROBLEMS

1. 28/112 is equivalent to 1:4

2. Maximum number of folders = (10)(25)(5) = 1250

3. Average annual increase = ($25,107-19,353) ÷ 7 = $822

4. $1,457,400 - (55)($16,800) = $533,400 = total amount paid to senior clerks. Average senior clerk's salary = $533,400 ÷ 28 = $19,050

5. Number of words on 3rd page = 954 - 283 - 366 = 305

6. Clerk A processed (40)(1.30) = 52 forms and clerk C processed (52)(1.25) = 65 forms. Finally, 65 - 40 = 25

7. Take-home pay = $678 - (.15)($678) - (.025)($678) - $1.95 - $9.00 = $548.40

8. (400)(12) = 4800 pencils. In 2002, (3/4)(4800) = 3600 were used, so that 1200 pencils were available at the beginning of 2003. Since 3600 pencils were also used in 2003, the agency had to buy 3600 - 1200 = 2400 pencils.

9. Average salary for clerk in Agency X = ($15,105+$15,750+$16,440)/3 = $15,765. Average salary for clerk in Agency Y = ($15,825+ $15,825+$16,086) ÷ 3 = $15,912. Difference in average salaries = $147.

10. Total pay = ($13.60)(40) + ($20.40)(5) = $646.00

11. In 2005, amount spent = $156,500 ÷ 1.12 ≈ $139,730 (Actual value = $139,732.1429)

12. At the end of 2 hours, (1100)(2) + (1450)(2) + (1200)(2) + (1300X2) + (1250X2) = 12,600 letters have been inserted into envelopes. The remaining 11,400 letters done by clerks A, B, and C will require 11,400 ÷ (1100+1450+1250) = 3 hours.

13. 60 ÷ .40 = 150

14. 96 ÷ 3/8 = (96)(8/3) = 256

15. Total cost = (5)[(25)(.20)+(35)(.30)+(350)(.40)]= $777.50

16. In 1998, (12,000) (1.25) = 15,000 applications were issued In 1996, (15,000)(.90) = 13,500 applications were issued

17. Total number of hours $=\dfrac{120}{40} + \dfrac{80}{20} = 7$

18. (.75)(500 dozen) = 375 dozen purchased in 2000 at a cost of ($1.20)(1.20) = $1.44 per dozen. Total cost for 2000 = ($1.44) (375) = $540

19. Total time = 1 hour + 450/75 hrs. = 7 hours

20. (.30)(420) - (1/7)(420) = 126 - 60 = 66

6 (#1)

21. Cost per minute = (120)(.02) = $2.40. Then, $12 ÷ $2.40 = 5 minutes

22. (32)(22) ÷ 16 = 44 clerks

23. Total amount paid = (20)($27,500)(2/12) + (18)($31,500)(4/12) + (22)($30,000)(3/12) = $445,666.$\overline{6}$ ≈ $450,000

24. Number of accountants with college degrees and five years of experience = (2300)(.05)(.80)(1/2) = 46

25. Let x = regular hourly pay. Then, (8)(x) + (1)(1.5x) = $1.71 So, 9.5x = 171. Solving, x = $18

TEST 2

DIRECTIONS: Each question or incomplete statement is followed by several suggested answers or completions. Select the one that BEST answers the question or completes the statement. *PRINT THE LETTER OF THE CORRECT ANSWER IN THE SPACE AT THE RIGHT.*

1. Assume that you know the capacity of a filing cabinet, the extent of which it is filled, and the daily rate at which material is being added to the file.
   In order to estimate how many more days it will take for the cabinet to be filled to capacity, you should

   A. divide the extent to which the cabinet is filled by the daily rate
   B. take the difference between the capacity of the cabinet and the material in it, and multiply the result by the daily rate of adding material
   C. divide the daily rate of adding material by the difference between the capacity of the cabinet and the material in it
   D. take the difference between the capacity of the cabinet and the material in it, and divide the result by the daily rate of adding material

   1.____

2. Suppose you have been asked to compute the average salary earned in your department during the past year. For each of the divisions of the department, you are given the number of employees and the average salary.
   In order to find the requested overall average salary for the department, you should

   A. add the average salaries of the various divisions and divide the total by the number of divisions
   B. multiply the number of employees in each division by the corresponding average salary, add the results and divide the total by the number of employees in the department
   C. add the average salaries of the various divisions and divide the total by the total number of employees in the department
   D. multiply the sum of the average salaries of the various divisions by the total number of divisions and divide the resulting product by the total number of employees in the department

   2.____

3. Suppose that a group of six clerks has been assigned to assemble the duplicated pages of a report into completed copies. After four hours of work, they have been able to complete one-third of the job.
   In order to assemble all the remaining copies in three more hours of work, the number of clerks which will have to be added to the original six, assuming that all the clerks assigned to this task work at the same rate of speed, is

   A. 10   B. 16   C. 2   D. 6

   3.____

4. A study of the grades of students in a certain college revealed that in 2005, 15% fewer students received a passing grade in mathematics than in 2004, whereas in 2006 the number of students passing mathematics increased 15% over 2005.
   On the basis of this study, it would be MOST accurate to conclude that

   A. the same percentage of students passed mathematics in 2004 as in 2006
   B. of the three years studied, the greatest percentage of students passed mathematics in 2006

   4.____

151

C. the percentage of students who passed mathematics in 2006 was less than the percentage passing this subject in 2004
D. the percentage of students passing mathematics in 2004 was 15% greater than the percentage of students passing this subject in 2006

5. A city department employs 1,400 people, of whom 35% are clerks and 1/8 are stenographers.
The number of employees in the department who are neither clerks nor stenographers is

   A. 640   B. 665   C. 735   D. 760

6. Assume that there are 190 papers to be filed and that Clerk A and Clerk B are assigned to file these papers. If Clerk A files 40 papers more than Clerk B, then the number of papers that Clerk A files is

   A. 75   B. 110   C. 115   D. 150

7. A stock clerk had on hand the following items:
   500 pads, each worth 16 cents
   130 pencils, each worth 12 cents
   50 dozen rubber bands, worth 8 cents a dozen
   If, from this stock, he issued 125 pads, 45 pencils, and 48 rubber bands, the value of the remaining stock would be

   A. $25.72   B. $27.80   C. $70.52   D. $73.88

8. In a particular agency, there were 160 accidents in 2002. Of these accidents, 75% were due to unsafe acts and the rest were due to unsafe conditions. In the following year, a special safety program was established. The number of accidents in 2004 due to unsafe acts was reduced to 35% of what it had been in 2002.
How many accidents due to unsafe acts were there in 2004?

   A. 20   B. 36   C. 42   D. 56

9. At the end of every month, the petty cash fund of Agency A is reimbursed for payments made from the fund during the month. During the month of February, the amounts paid from the fund were entered on receipts as follows: 10 bus fares of $1.40 each and one taxi fare of $14.00. At the end of the month, the money left in the fund was in the following denominations: 60 one-dollar bills, 16 quarters, 40 dimes, and 80 nickels.
If the petty cash fund is reduced by 20% for the following month, how much money will there be available in the petty cash fund for March?

   A. $44   B. $80   C. $86   D. $100

10. An employee worked on a job for 6 weeks, 5 days per week, and 8 hours per day. How many hours did he work on the job?

    A. 40   B. 48   C. 55   D. 240

11. Divide 35 by .7.

    A. 5   B. 42   C. 50   D. 245

12. .1% of 25 =

   A. .025   B. .25   C. 2.5   D. 25

13. In a city agency, 80 percent of the total number of employees are more than 25 years of age and 65 percent of the total number of employees are high school graduates.
   The SMALLEST possible percent of employees who are both high school graduates and more than 25 years of age is

   A. 35%   B. 45%   C. 55%   D. 65%

14. Two clerical units, X and Y, each having a different number of clerks, are assigned to file registration cards. It takes Unit X, which contains 8 clerks, 21 days to file the same number of cards that Unit Y can file in 28 days. It is also a fact that Unit X can file 174,528 cards in 72 days.
   Assuming that all the clerks in both units work at the same rate of speed, the number of cards which can be filed by Unit Y in 144 days, if 4 more clerks are added to the staff of Unit Y, is MOST NEARLY

   A. 392,000   B. 436,000   C. 523,000   D. 669,000

15. Assume that two machines, each costing $14,750, were purchased for your office. Each machine requires the services of an operator at a salary of $2,000 per month. These machines are to replace six clerks, two of whom earn $1,550 per month each, and four of whom earn $1,700 per month each.
   The number of months it will take for the cost of the machines to be made up from the savings in salaries is

   A. less than four   B. four
   C. five   D. more than five

16. Suppose that the amount of stationery used by your department in August decreased by 16% as compared with the amount used in July, and that the amount used in September increased by 25% as compared with the amount used in August.
   The amount of stationery used in September as compared with the amount used in July is

   A. greater by 5 percent   B. less by 5 percent
   C. greater by 9 percent   D. the same

17. An employee earns $48 a day and works 5 days a week.
   He will earn $2,160 in _____ weeks.

   A. 5   B. 7   C. 8   D. 9

18. In a certain bureau, the entire staff consists of 1 senior supervisor, 2 supervisors, 6 assistant supervisors, and 54 associate workers.
   The percent of the staff who are not associate workers is MOST NEARLY

   A. 14   B. 21   C. 27   D. 32

19. In a certain bureau, five employees each earn $1,000 a month, another 3 employees each earn $2,200 a month, and another two employees each earn $1,400 a month.
   The monthly payroll for these employees is

   A. $3,600   B. $8,800   C. $11,400   D. $14,400

20. An employee contributes 5% of his salary to the pension fund. If his salary is $1,200 a month, the amount of his contribution to the pension fund in a year is

   A. $480   B. $720   C. $960   D. $1,200

21. The number of square feet in an area that is 50 feet long and 30 feet wide is

   A. 80   B. 150   C. 800   D. 1,500

22. A farm hand was paid a weekly wage of $332.16 for a 48-hour work week. As a result of a new labor contract, he is paid $344.96 a week for a 44-hour work week with time and one-half pay for time worked in excess of 44 hours in any work week.
    If he continues to work 48 hours weekly under the new contract, the amount by which his average hourly rate for a 48-hour work week under the new contract exceeds the hourly rate previously paid him lies between _____ and _____ cents, inclusive.

   A. 91;100   B. 101;110   C. 111;120   D. 121;130

23. Each side of a square room, which is being used as an office, measures 66 feet. The floor of the room is divided by six traffic aisles, each aisle being six feet wide. Three of the aisles run parallel to the east and west sides of the room, and the other three run parallel to the north and south sides of the room, so that the remaining floor space is divided into 16 equal sections. If all of the floor space which is not being used for traffic aisles is occupied by desk and chair sets, and each set takes up 24 square feet of floor space, the number of desk and chair sets in the room is

   A. 80   B. 64   C. 36   D. 96

24. In 2005, a city agency bought 12,000 envelopes at $4.00 per hundred. In 2006, the price of envelopes purchased was 40 percent higher than the 2005 price, but only 60 percent as many envelopes were bought.
    The total cost of the envelopes purchased in 2006 was MOST NEARLY

   A. $250   B. $320   C. $400   D. $480

25. In a city agency, 25 percent of the women employees and 50 percent of the men employees attended a general staff meeting.
    If 48 percent of all the employees in the agency are women, the percentage of all the employees who attended the meeting is

   A. 36%   B. 37%   C. 38%   D. 75%

KEY (CORRECT ANSWERS)

1. D
2. B
3. A
4. C
5. C

6. C
7. D
8. C
9. B
10. D

11. C
12. A
13. B
14. A
15. C

16. A
17. D
18. A
19. D
20. B

21. D
22. D
23. D
24. C
25. C

SOLUTIONS TO PROBLEMS

1. To determine number of days required to fill cabinet to capacity, subtract material in it from capacity amount, then divide by daily rate of adding material. Example: A cabinet already has 10 folders in it, and the capacity is 100 folders. Suppose 5 folders per day are added. Number of days to fill to capacity = (100-10) ÷ 5 = 18

2. To determine overall average salary, multiply number of employees in each division by that division's average salary, add results, then divide by total number of employees. Example: Division A has 4 employees with average salary of $40,000; division B has 6 employees with average salary of $36,000; division C has 2 employees with average salary of $46,000. Average salary = [(4)($40,000)+(6)($36,000)+(2)($46,000)] / 12 = $39,000

3. (6)(4) = 24 clerk-hours. Since only one-third of work has been done, (24) (3) - 24 = 48 clerk-hours remain. Then, 48 3 = 16 clerks. Thus, 16 - 6 = 10 additional clerks.

4. The percentage of students passing math in 2006 was less than the percentage of those passing math in 2004. Example: Suppose 400 students passed math in 2004. Then, (400)(.85) = 340 passed in 2005. Finally, (340)(1.15) = 391 passed in 2006.

5. 1400 - (.35)(1400) - (1/8)(1400) = 735

6. Let x = number of papers filed by clerk A, x-40 = number of papers filed by clerk B. Then, x + (x-40) = 190 Solving, x = 115

7. (500-125)(.16) + (130-45)(.12) + (50 - 48/12)(.08) = $60.00 + $10.20 + $3.68 = $73.88

8. (160)(.75) = 120 accidents due to unsafe acts in 2002. In 2004, (120)(.35) = 42 accidents due to unsafe acts

9. Original amount at beginning of February in the fund = (10)($1.40) + (1)($14.00) + (60)($1) + (16)(.25) + (40)(.10) + (80)(.05) = $100. Finally, for March, ($100)(.80) = $80 will be available

10. Total hours = (6)(5)(8) = 240

11. 35 ÷ .7 = 50

12. .1% of 25 = (.001)(25) = .025

13. Let A = percent of employees who are at least 25 years old and B = percent of employees who are high school graduates. Also, let N = percent of employees who fit neither category and J = percent of employees who are in both categories.
Then, 100 = A + B + N - J. Substituting, 100 = 80 + 65 + N - J To minimize J, let N = 0. So, 100 = 80 + 65 + 0 - J. Solving, J = 45

14. Let Y = number of clerks in Unit Y. Then, (8)(21) = (4)(28), so Y = 6. Unit X has 8 clerks who can file 174,528 cards in 72 flays; thus, each clerk in Unit X can file 174,528 ÷ 72 ÷ 8 = 303 cards per day. Adding 4 clerks to Unit Y will yield 10 clerks in that unit. Since their rate is equal to that of Unit X, the clerks in Unit Y will file, in 144 days, is (303)(10)(144) = 436,320 ≈ 436,000 cards.

15. Let x = required number of months. The cost of the machines in x months = (2)(14,750) + (2)(2000)(x) = 29,500 + 4000x. The savings in salaries for the displaced clerks = x[(2)(1550) +(4)(1700)] = 9900x. Thus, 29,500 + 4000x = 9900x. Solving, x = 5. So, five months will elapse in order to achieve a savings in cost.

16. Let x = amount used in July, so that .84x = amount used in August. For September, the amount used = (.84x)(1.25) = 1.05x. This means the amount used in September is 5% more than the amount used in July.

17. Each week he earns ($48)(5) = $240. Then, $2160 ÷ $240 = 9 weeks

18. (1+2+6) ÷ 63 = 1/7 ≈ 14%

19. Monthly payroll = (5)($1000) + (3)($2200) + (2)($1400) = $14,400

20. Yearly contribution to pension fund = (12)($1200)(.05) = $720

21. (50')(30') = 1500 sq.ft.

22. Old rate = 332.16 ÷ 48 = 6.92 (48 hours)
    New rate = 344.96 (44 hours)
    Overtime rate = 344.96 ÷ 44 = 7.75/hr. x 1.5 x 4 = 46.48
    344.96 + 46.48 = 391.44
    391.44 ÷ 48 = 8.15
    815 - 692 = 123 cents an hour more

23. Each of the 16 sections is a square with side [66'-(3)(6')] ÷ 4 = 12'. So each section contains (12')(12') = 144 sq.ft.
    The number of desk and chair sets = (144 ÷ 24) (16) = 96

24. In 2006, (.60)(12,000) = 7200 envelopes were bought and the price per hundred was ($4.00)(1.40) = $5.60. The total cost = (5.60)(72) = $403.20 ≈ $400

25. (.25)(.48) + (.50)(.52) = .38 = 38%

TEST 3

DIRECTIONS: Each question or incomplete statement is followed by several suggested answers or completions. Select the one that BEST answers the question or completes the statement. *PRINT THE LETTER OF THE CORRECT ANSWER IN THE SPACE AT THE RIGHT.*

1. According to one suggested filing system, no more than 12 folders should be filed behind any one file guide and from 10 to 20 file guides should be used in each file drawer. Based on this filing system, the MAXIMUM number of folders that a four-drawer file cabinet can hold is

    A. 240   B. 480   C. 960   D. 1,200

    1.____

2. A certain office uses three different forms. Last year, it used 3,500 copies of Form L, 6,700 copies of Form M, and 10,500 copies of Form P. This year, the office expects to decrease the use of each of these forms by 5%. The TOTAL number of these three forms which the office expects to use this year is

    A. 10,350   B. 16,560   C. 19,665   D. 21,735

    2.____

3. The hourly rate of pay for a certain part-time employee is computed by dividing his yearly salary rate by the number of hours in the work year. The employee's yearly salary rate is $18,928, and there are 1,820 hours in the work year.
   If this employee works 18 hours during one week, his TOTAL earnings for these 18 hours are

    A. $180.00   B. $183.60   C. $187.20   D. $190.80

    3.____

4. Assume that the regular work week of an employee is 35 hours and that the employee is paid for any extra hours worked according to the following schedule. For hours worked in excess of 35 hours, up to and including 40 hours, the employee receives his regular hourly rate of pay. For hours worked in excess of 40 hours, the employee receives 1 1/2 times his hourly rate of pay.
   If the employee's hourly rate of pay is $11.20 and he works 43 hours during a certain week, his TOTAL pay for the week would be

    A. $481.60   B. $498.40   C. $556.00   D. $722.40

    4.____

5. A clerk divided his 35 hour work week as follows:
    1/5 of his time in sorting mail;
    1/2 of his time in filing letters; and
    1/7 of his time in reception work.
   The rest of his time was devoted to messenger work. The percentage of time spent on messenger work by the clerk during the week was MOST NEARLY

    A. 6%   B. 10%   C. 14%   D. 16%

    5.____

6. A city department has set up a computing unit and has rented 5 computing machines at a yearly rental of $700 per machine. In addition, the cost to the department for the maintenance and repair of each of these machines is $50 per year. Five computing machine operators, each receiving an annual salary of $15,000, and a supervisor, who receives $19,000 a year, have been assigned to this unit. This unit will perform the work previously performed by 10 employees whose combined salary was $162,000 a year.
   On the basis of these facts, the savings that will result from the operation of this computing unit for 5 years will be MOST NEARLY

    A. $250,000   B. $320,000   C. $330,000   D. $475,000

    6.____

7. Twelve clerks are assigned to enter certain data on index cards. This number of clerks could perform the task in 18 days. After these clerks have worked on this assignment for 6 days, 4 more clerks are added to the staff to do this work.
   Assuming that all the clerks work at the same rate of speed, the entire task, instead of taking 18 days, will be performed in _____ days.

   A. 9   B. 12   C. 15   D. 16

8. Suppose that a file cabinet, which has a capacity of 3,000 cards, now contains approximately 2,200 cards. Cards are added to the file at the average rate of 30 cards a day.
   To find the number of days it will take to fill the cabinet to capacity,

   A. divide 3,000 by 30
   B. divide 2,200 by 3,000
   C. divide 800 by 30
   D. multiply 30 by the fraction 2,200 divided by 3,000

9. Six gross of special drawing pencils were purchased for use in a city department.
   If the pencils were used at the rate of 24 a week, the MAXIMUM number of weeks that the six gross of pencils would last is _____ weeks.

   A. 6   B. 12   C. 24   D. 36

10. A stock clerk had 600 pads on hand. He then issued 3/8 of his supply of pads to Division X, 1/4 to Division Y, and 1/6 to Division Z.
    The number of pads remaining in stock is

    A. 48   B. 125   C. 240   D. 475

11. If a certain job can be performed by 18 clerks in 26 days, the number of clerks needed to perform the job in 12 days is _____ clerks.

    A. 24   B. 30   C. 39   D. 52

12. In anticipation of a seasonal increase in the amount of work to be performed by his division, a division chief prepared the following list of additional temporary employees needed by his division and the amount of time they would be employed:
        26 cashiers, each at $24,000 a year, for 2 months
        15 laborers, each at $85.00 a day, for 50 days
        6 clerks, each at $21,000 a year, for 3 months
    The total approximate cost for this additional personnel would be MOST NEARLY

    A. $200,000   B. $250,000   C. $500,000   D. $600,000

13. A copy machine company offered to sell a city agency 4 copy machines at a discount of 15% from the list price, and to allow the agency $850 for each of its two old machines. The list price of the new machines is $6,250 per machine.
    If the city agency accepts this offer, the amount of money it will have to provide for the purchase of these 4 machines is

    A. $17,350   B. $22,950   C. $19,550   D. $18,360

14. A stationery buyer was offered bond paper at the following price scale:
    $1.43 per ream for the first 1,000 reams
    $1.30 per ream for the next 4,000 reams
    $1.20 per ream for each additional ream beyond 5,000 reams
    If the buyer ordered 10,000 reams of paper, the average cost per ream, computed to the nearest cent, was

    A. $1.24   B. $1.26   C. $1.31   D. $1.36

15. A clerk has 5.70 percent of his salary deducted for his retirement pension. If this clerk's annual salary is $20,400, the monthly deduction for his retirement pension is

    A. $298.20   B. $357.90   C. $1,162.80   D. $96.90

16. In a certain bureau, two-thirds of the employees are clerks and the remainder are typists. If there are 90 clerks, then the number of typists in this bureau is

    A. 135   B. 45   C. 120   D. 30

17. The number of investigations conducted by an agency in 1999 was 3,600. In 2000, the number of investigations conducted was one-third more than in 1999. The number of investigations conducted in 2001 was three-fourths of the number conducted in 2000. It is anticipated that the number of investigations conducted in 2002 will be equal to the average of the three preceding years. On the basis of this information, the MOST accurate of the following statements is that the number of investigations conducted in

    A. 1999 is larger than the number anticipated for 2002
    B. 2000 is smaller than the number anticipated for 2002
    C. 2001 is equal to the number conducted in 1999
    D. 2001 is larger than the number anticipated in 2002

18. A city agency engaged in repair work uses a small part which the city purchases for 14 each. Assume that, in a certain year, the total expenditure of the city for this part was $700.
    How many of these parts were purchased that year?

    A. 50   B. 200   C. 2,000   D. 5,000

19. The work unit which you supervise is responsible for processing 15 reports per month. If your unit has 4 clerks and the best worker completes 40% of the reports himself, how many reports would each of the other clerks have to complete if they all do an equal number?

    A. 1   B. 2   C. 3   D. 4

20. Assume that the work unit in which you work has 24 clerks and 18 stenographers. In order to change the ratio of stenographers to clerks so that there is 1 stenographer for every 4 clerks, it would be necessary to REDUCE the number of stenographers by

    A. 3 B. 6 C. 9 D. 12

21. The arithmetic mean salary for five employees earning $18,500, $18,300, $18,600, $18,400, and $18,500, respectively, is

    A. $18,450 B. $18,460 C. $18,475 D. $18,500

22. Last year, a city department which is responsible for purchasing supplies ordered bond paper in equal quantities from 22 different companies. The price was exactly the same for each company, and the total cost for the 22 orders was $693,113.
    Assuming prices did not change during the year, the cost of each order was MOST NEARLY

    A. $31,490 B. $31,495 C. $31,500 D. $31,505

23. Suppose that a large bureau has 187 employees. On a particular day, approximately 14% of these employees are not available for work because of absences due to vacation, illness, or other reasons. Of the remaining employees, 1/7 are assigned to a special project while the balance are assigned to the normal work of the bureau. The number of employees assigned to the normal work of the bureau on that day is

    A. 112 B. 124 C. 138 D. 142

24. Suppose that you are in charge of a typing pool of 8 typists. Two typists type at the rate of 38 words per minute; three type at the rate of 40 words per minute; three type at the rate of 42 words per minute. The average typewritten page consists of 50 lines, 12 words per line. Each employee works from 9 to 5 with one hour off for lunch.
    The total number of pages typed by this pool in one day is, on the average, CLOSEST to _____ pages.

    A. 205 B. 225 C. 250 D. 275

25. Suppose that part-time workers are paid $7.20 an hour, prorated to the nearest half hour, with pay guaranteed for a minimum of four hours if services are required for less than four hours. In one operation, part-time workers signed the time sheet as follows:

Worker	In	Out
A	8:00 A.M.	11:35 A.M.
B	8:30 A.M.	3:20 P.M.
C	7:55 A.M.	11:00 A.M.
D	8:30 A.M.	2:25 P.M.

    How much would TOTAL payment to these part-time workers amount to for this operation, assuming that those who stayed after 12 Noon were not paid for one hour which they took off for lunch?

    A. $134.40 B. $136.80 C. $142.20 D. $148.80

KEY (CORRECT ANSWERS)

1. C
2. C
3. C
4. B
5. D

6. B
7. C
8. C
9. D
10. B

11. C
12. A
13. C
14. B
15. D

16. B
17. C
18. D
19. C
20. D

21. B
22. D
23. C
24. B
25. B

---

6 (#3)

SOLUTIONS TO PROBLEMS

1. Maximum number of folders = (4)(12)(20) = 960

2. (3500+6700+10,500)(.95) = 19,665

3. Hourly rate = $18,928 ÷ 1820 = $10.40. Then, the pay for 18 hours = ($10.40)(18) = $187.20

4. Total pay = ($11.20)(40) + ($11.20)(1.5)(3) = $498.40

5. (1 - 1/5 - 1/2 - 1/7)(100)% ≈ 16%

6. Previous cost for five years = ($324,000)(5) = $1,620,000
   Present cost for five years = (5)(5)($1,400) + (5)(5)($100) + (5)(5)($30,000) + (1)(5)($38,000) = $977,500   The net savings = $642,500 ≈ $640,000

7. (12)(18) = 216 clerk-days. Then, 216 - (12)(6) = 144 clerk-days of work left when 4 more clerks are added. Now, 16 clerks will finish the task in 144 ÷ 16 = 9 more days. Finally, the task will require a total of 6 + 9 = 15 days.

8. Number of days needed = (3000-2200) ÷ 30 = 26.7, which is equivalent to dividing 800 by 30.

9. (6)(144) = 864 pencils purchased. Then, 864 ÷ 24 = 36 maximum number of weeks

10. Number of remaining pads = 600 - (1)(600) - (1/4)(600) - (1/6)(600) = 125

11. (18)(26) ÷ 12 = 39 clerks

12. Total cost = (26)($24,000)(2/12) + (15)($85)(50) + (6)($21,000)(3/12) = $199,250 $200,000

13. (4)($6250)(.85) - (2)($850) = $19,550

14. Total cost = ($1.43)(1000) + ($1.30)(4000) + ($1.20X5000) = $12,630. Average cost per ream = $12,630 10,000 ≈ $1.26

15. Monthly salary = $20,400 ÷ 12 = $1700. Thus, the monthly deduction for his pension = ($1700)(.057) + $96.90

16. Number of employees = 90 ÷ 2/3 = 135. Then, the number of typists = (1/3)(135) = 45

17. The number of investigations for each year is as follows:
    1999: 3600
    2000: (3600)(1 1/3) = 4800
    2001: (4800)(3/4) = 3600
    2002: (3600+4800+3600)/3 = 4000
    So, the number of investigations were equal for 1999 and 2001.

18. $700 ÷ .14 = 5000 parts

19. The best worker does (.40)(15) = 6 reports. The other 9 reports are divided equally among the other 3 clerks, so each clerk does 9 ÷ 3 = 3 reports.

20. 1:4 = 6:24 . Thus, the number of stenographers must be reduced by 18 - 6 = 12

21. Mean = ($18,500+$18,300+$18,400+$18,500) ÷ 5 = $18,460

22. The cost per order = $693,113 ÷ 22 ≈ $31,505

23. 187 - (.14) = 26. 187 - 26 = 161 - 1/7 (161) = 23
    161 - 23 = 138

24. Number of words typed in 1 min. = (2)(38) + (3)(40) + (3)(42) = 322. For 7 hours, the total number of words typed = (7)(60)(322) = 135,240. Each page contains (on the average) (50)(12) = 600 words. Finally, 135,240 ÷ 600 ≈ 225 pages

25. Worker A = ($7.20)(4) = $28.80
    Worker B = ($7.20)(3 1/2) + ($7.20)(2 1/2) = $43.20
    Worker C = ($7.20)(4) = $28.80
    Worker D = ($7.20)(3 1/2) + ($7.20)(1 1/2) = $36.00
    Total for all 4 workers = $136.80
    Note: Workers A and C received the guaranteed minimum 4 hours pay each.

www.ingramcontent.com/pod-product-compliance
Lightning Source LLC
Chambersburg PA
CBHW082121230426
43671CB00015B/2762